The Country Antique Dealer

The Country Antique Dealer

With a Gazetteer of Market Towns and Auctioneers in the
United Kingdom

Peter Austen

Illustrations by Leslie Atkinson

DAVID & CHARLES
Newton Abbot   London   North Pomfret (Vt)

Dedicated to Bruce and Linda for their encouragement

British Library Cataloguing in Publication Data

Austen, Peter
  The country antique dealer.
  1. Antique dealers – Great Britain
  I. Title
  380.1'457451'0941   NK928

  ISBN 0–7153–8223–3

Photoset by
Northern Phototypesetting Co. Bolton
and printed in Great Britain
by Redwood Burn Ltd. Trowbridge Wilts.
for David & Charles (Publishers) Limited
Brunel House Newton Abbot Devon

Published in the United States of America
by David & Charles Inc.
North Pomfret Vermont 05053 USA

Contents

Prologue

A short time ago a painting by John Constable was sold in a major London saleroom for the ridiculous sum of £38 (plus, of course, 10 per cent service charge and 15 per cent VAT). Neither the auctioneers nor the bidders in the room knew that it was a Constable, so it was sold for the also-ran price that a competent but fairly nondescript painting of the English school, early nineteenth century, would fetch in a London saleroom. In these salerooms most of the buyers are quite happy to pay top money for well authenticated pictures, at the same time taking a rather high-handed and short-sighted attitude to what appear to be the more humble entries in the sale. So no one except a certain Nicholas Drummond, who simply happened to like it, paid the little landscape (approximately 9in by 6in) much attention. That's why it went for a song.

The painting had come from a house clearance in Colchester, where it was removed from a cellar by a couple who inherited both house and contents which they proceeded to sell through the auction houses. Nicholas Drummond, who had snapped up the painting in the London rooms, sold it for £150 to his brother William who, after much detective work, had it authenticated as a genuine John Constable.

An even shorter time ago an old flower pot which was often left standing to catch the rain outside a West Country bungalow was sold by Sotheby's in London for £265,000. Not, you will understand, because of any acute shortage of bowls in which to grow plants, but because the flower pot happened to have been made in China during the fifteenth century in the Ming Dynasty, which was always a good period for the manufacture of blue and white flower pots! Needless to say, the widow who was using this classical piece of porcelain, about 6½ins in diameter, for propagation purposes was blissfully unaware of its provenance and value until it was spotted by a Sotheby's expert whom the lady called in to value a picture she owned. Which is undoubtedly just as well, otherwise she would probably have dropped it with fright years ago. Now the bowl, one of only three known to exist, has brought the lady a football pools-size fortune without the tedium of having to study form. Let us hope she has bought some nice plants with the money.

These incidents have only confirmed that involvement with the world of antiques is one of the most delightful, rewarding, surprising, and sometimes amusing pursuits a person can follow.

It was a world I entered myself in the early 1970s, quite by chance. Frankly, I didn't know the difference between a commode and a cheese-dish when I started. But I became so captivated by the adventurous new horizons that were opened up to me that I became a dealer in antiques and a visitor to a world of characters of whom a novelist would be proud.

In the last seven years or so I have secured some amazing bargains and enjoyed and shared a great deal of good humour with the people I have met. I have learnt about the antiques game the hard way, gaining first-hand knowledge of some of the roguery and mischief which sometimes goes on. I've been up to a few tricks myself, I must admit.

If you thought the antiques game was solely for the serious, the monied, the expert or the just plain lucky, let me tell you how the excitement, the humour – and occasionally the money – came my way when I became involved with the mystique of antique dealing and collecting. I entered a colourful world full of unusual characters. In this book I shall visit some of them again.

Stowmarket, Suffolk. August, 1981

1
Cottage Industry

I acquired my taste for antiques along with an appetite for goats' milk, redcurrants and fresh-killed rabbits. For all these things were available every Tuesday in a Kentish country market where the quality of carrots, cattle or collectables was always likely to be variable but where value for money was a constant attraction.

In this market town Mr Moses was the red-faced and avuncular auctioneer who filled his two sheds each week with local produce and antique and household goods, all drawn from a catchment area of about twenty miles' radius. Every week I and a few dozen others would push our way round his dusty huts among the boiling hens and trays of cracked eggs, the secondhand bicycles and Victorian prints in maple frames, looking for bargains at the bottom of an orange box or the genuine sovereign skilfully hidden by local dealers in the corner of a grandmother's purse full of old coins.

Anything was likely to turn up, and almost invariably did. Stacked in every available nook and cranny of the auction room were cookers and fridges, wellington boots and chicken wire, oil paintings and oleographs, sets of Victorian dining chairs and piles of secondhand clothes. There was junk jewellery and the occasional diamond brooch, gold rings and curtain rings, amateur pictures of the local parish church and a genuine Birkett Foster. And scrambling among these goodies were diddicoys and dole malingerers, housewives and harlots, schoolboys and teddy-boys, dealers and dabblers. In fact, all human life was there. And they came every Tuesday, sharp-eyed and hamburger-munching, ready for the killing that would mean prosperity for a week and the satisfaction of being one-up on the smart neighbours who commuted to London every day.

The first time I went I knew very little about antiques and was also a bit naive about man's inhumanity to man. For you had to be a bit tough and aggressive to shove your way through the sweating bodies pawing through the rubbish in their search for the odd treasure or two that was there for the finding every week. And when the time came to bid for what had taken your fancy, you had to be sure you got right in front of the auctioneer's chair, which was precariously balanced on an old pine table. If you were not right in front the lot would be knocked down to one of the regulars and no amount of disputing that you were still bidding would ever induce the perspiring auctioneer to put the lot up again.

But within a week or two the techniques had been acquired and, such was the shifting population of a country market, a couple of weeks' visits established you as one of the regulars.

That meant Mr Moses would no longer ignore you: in fact his eye would seek yours, and it seemed that if it was your 'turn' a lot would be yours despite continued bidding by a newcomer in the back of the room.

One hot summer morning, when perspiration and ill-temper were around in equal measure, a short, fat man with ginger hair and a temperament to match disputed a lot with the auctioneer, insisting he had still been bidding when it was knocked down to Lofty, a regular and very favoured client. Mr Moses, who was equally portly, rather redder in the face and with muscles developed by years of auctioneering in the often less salubrious salerooms of Kent, leaped from his precarious rostrum to remonstrate with the heckler. For such a large man he could move amazingly quickly. He sprang from the pine table, scattering small boys and jardinières in his wake, grabbed the by now ashen buyer by the lapels of a Harris tweed jacket that had seen better days, lifted him bodily from the ground and dumped him outside the hut like a sack of potatoes. The technique had no doubt been learned in the produce hut next door, where many hundredweights of spuds had been sold by the redoubtable Moses.

'Get out of my saleroom and never come back,' said Moses. And that's all he said. He just left the man there on the concrete, mouth agape and a look of total disbelief and misery on his face. Mr Moses re-entered the saleroom with considerable dignity, made his way back to the rostrum along an aisle respectfully made for him by a now silent and awestruck crowd, and clambered back on to his stool.

'Lot 39, the stationery box; do I see 20p?' he said, as though all that sort of palaver were part of a normal day's business. Which perhaps, in that place, it was.

I never saw anyone give Moses any trouble after that. For weeks afterwards bidding was conducted in an exemplary fashion by the regulars, although all sorts of grave injustices were perpetrated by Moses without a sign of demur from anyone. Nobody fancied being dumped on the concrete; and besides, no one with any sense was going to be denied the chance of making some real money out of the occasional very good buy indeed that was there every week at 'The Tatty'.

11

As for that 20p for a stationery box, yes, that really was the starting price − twenty *pence*. And this was at a time when a reasonably posh dealer would be selling one of these pretty little Victorian boxes − the ones with a writing slope and ink-wells inside and a bit of marquetry on the lid − for anything from £15 to £25, depending on quality. The bidding on such an item would progress in 10p stages up to £1, and then, with the 'big boys' on it, by positive leaps of 25p a time up to an eventual selling price, so far as this box was concerned, of £3.25. It was then no trouble to sell the item for £5.50 or £6 to a local dealer slightly higher up the hierarchy, who would then sell it to his trade buyer for a tenner. And so on up through the trade.

I can only remember two occasions when Mr Moses began the bidding at the inflated level of £1. Once was for a small George I oak bureau, 2ft 6in wide, which was half hidden under some old carpets in a corner of the saleroom. True, there was a drawer missing and a brass drop handle was off, but it was worth £200 of anybody's money and eventually sold for £45, which caused quite a stir among the ignorant, who thought it was a broken kiddies' desk. Mr Moses knew perfectly well what it was, and what it was worth, but he confessed to me once that his great pleasure in life was making money for people.

The other occasion when the bidding started at £1 was on an item I had entered in the sale myself. One of the ways you could ingratiate yourself with Mr Moses was by becoming a regular vendor as well as a buyer, so within a few weeks I was entering a dozen or so lots each Tuesday. Nothing very exciting: a box or two of books, some Kilner jars, reproduction pot lids (they really caused a bit of excitement among the ignorant, who thought they were the real thing and insisted on paying £4 to £5 each for them; ah, well, it's an ill wind). That was the sort of stuff. Except that this particular week I entered a stag's head, a really nice stag's head with seven points and excellent quality glass eyes. I had bought it a week before at a country house sale for £5. No dealer would really want such a thing and private buyers were not prepared to put their money where their deer-stalkers were; so I got it cheap.

It was hung above Mr Moses' head on the rostrum, where among the tat of the Tuesday hut it looked grand and very

12

desirable. Remembering the incident of the Harris tweed clad bidder, I hoped Moses wouldn't grab it to make a point to someone on that particular day! Before the sale there had been whispers among the diddicoys as to how much it might fetch. 'Twenty quid,' I heard from one. 'No, it's worth a lot more than that,' said someone else. So I was expecting big things. I had put a reserve of £10 on it. Seeing this on his sale sheet, Mr Moses was obviously agonised as to how he would ever obtain such a sum.

'Now the stag's head,' he said. 'It's a beauty. Best one we've ever had. Do I see £1?'

Quite clearly he hadn't, because he then started plucking bids from the wall like a starving man grabbing apples in a Kentish orchard. From the back to the front of the room went Moses' eyes, almost faster than you could follow, and no sooner had you turned to see who could be bidding than he was off on a flight of fancy to another part of the room and, unless you knew his ways, there was no means of telling whether they were genuine or all quite spurious. On and on the bids went by unprecedented 50p jumps and gradually the auctioneer's pseudo-excitement caught on among the slower witted in the room and at £11 a housewife in front of me made a bid which Moses took in with the corner of his twinkling eye. From then on there was no hope for the poor dear. Using an indifferent farmer at the back of the room who stood with mouth agape as Moses plucked bids from him, the lady was nodding on the pounds and the farmer was being used for the fifty pences. Up soared the price, £17, £18, £19, and then it was hers at £20.

She looked pleased, and I hope she was. She had certainly taken part in a wonderful performance; Olivier himself might have been proud of it. I was delighted. Mr Moses took his 20 per cent (yes, a high rate of commission, but when he was selling at such low sums it was the only way the poor chap could eat) and I made £11 clear profit on the stag's head which, a week before, nobody had wanted.

Tuesdays at Moses' auction room would seem to have epitomised the dealer's dream of buying cheap and selling dear – up to a point. It is true that a tyro like myself could make the occasional killing, but there were two or three other dealers there most weeks who, with cash and experience, could see off the

13

amateur if they had set their hearts on something.

Lofty was the local shipper: he bought most of the Victorian-to-early Twenties furniture, including wardrobes, and shipped it from his local barn to trade contacts in the United States. Anything that smacked of better quality 'Viccy' (as I learnt to call Victorian pieces) would almost always be his. Then there was 'Jim', who worked under a variety of pseudonyms. He knew much about the cheaper end of the trade, and quite a bit about the better stuff; any lack of knowledge was compensated for by innate cunning and plenty of contacts who would see him out of the occasional bit of trouble. What Lofty missed or did not want, 'Jim' would buy and pass on to the next link in the buying chain; or he would salt it away in his own private horde of things he had acquired on the cheap.

My third greatest rival was a woman called Bessie, who was large and smoked heavily on long black cheroots. She always wore an old fur coat stained with various saleroom adventures, had fat red legs with a rash and wore no stockings. I never saw her dressed any other way, summer or winter, and always under that fur coat was an enormous bulge around the midriff. She was too old to be pregnant, and initially I felt sorry about what I imagined was a very painful ovarian cyst condition. Eventually, the more I learned about Bessie the more convinced I became that the bulge was in fact a pouch into which could be secreted all manner of goodies. She was a fly old bird and one ended up having something approaching admiration for her. With no more than a very basic smattering of knowledge, but with an obvious eye for a fast buck, she used her bulk and rather unpleasant smell to push her way to within close bidding distance of Moses' rostrum. I discovered where she sold the stuff again one day at a high-quality sale held regularly by another firm of local auctioneers, when items Bessie had acquired at 'The Tatty' were bought by London dealers for four or five times what she had paid for them. Except in the hot weather, there were no flies on Bessie!

Apart from these local rivals, I encountered another problem. There seemed to be a grapevine of information (maybe set up by Moses himself) which meant that wealthier dealers from quite a wide area always seemed to know when the auctioneer had a good house-clearance lot in. Moses had an arrangement with a local removal company, it appeared, so that when a deceased's home had to be cleared and the contents disposed of, Moses' saleroom was the place where it ended up. Every five weeks or so the removal firm's lorry would arrive at the market at about 7am to disgorge a houseful of often good-quality antique furniture, china, silver and paintings. The sale hut would be stacked to the roof with sets of chairs and a Georgian dining table or two, whatnots, a bookcase and bureau, cutlery, cookers, fridges and piles of junk from the attic of some local Edwardian house. And on such occasions Moses' hut would bristle with men in striped suits, smoking cigars, and lady dealers in flat country shoes.

I did not get a look in on those days and used to complain bitterly about the prices. A set of four Trafalgar-style dining chairs for £65 . . . a whatnot for £25 . . . a warming pan that fetched £15 . . . those three eighteenth-century English school oils of racehorses that fetched £40 each! To me, that was lunacy. What is clear now, though, is that *I* was the madman – for not buying the lot. Everything that was sold that day probably eventually retailed for five times what those dealers paid. But I was wet behind the ears in those days of 1973.

Wet or not, however, I still managed to buy quite well. Looking through my stockbook for that year, I found an entry for a typical Tuesday morning's purchases. They make interesting reading and I only wish I could replace them today, even at four times the price:

	£
Marble clock with French movement	3.50
Box assorted china	20
Box old 78 records and qty pianola rolls	75
Three oil paintings	8.25
American wall clock	14.50
Antique trunk bearing Victorian train labels	1.50
Victorian duchess dressing table	3.50
Gladstone bag	35
Set 4 Victorian walnut dining chairs on cabriole legs	30.00
Three Bentwood chairs	1.50
Benares brass tray and stand	4.50
Roll-top Edwardian bureau	10.00

Most of those items you can still find today at reasonable cost. The marble mantel clock on heavy base with square hood was difficult to shift at more than a fiver. Even today these clocks are sold for only £20 or so, although in my view they are bound to go up in price when their basic quality is appreciated. Marble itself is expensive enough if you try to buy some; and the movements of these clocks were usually imported from France and were of excellent quality, being used in much more expensive clocks than the marble ones. So even if you really detest the case itself, the works are worth keeping against the day something more exotic in ormolu and tortoiseshell turns up with a broken movement. The mechanism from the marble timepiece will probably fit.

The American wall clock – in rosewood case with a painted scene of a US railroad under the dial and about 3ft high – was also a bit of a drag on the market at the time. Such clocks had very reliable movements but I always found the cases rather vulgar, ugly and difficult to get rid of in the trade. They were imported by the thousand into Britain from the USA during late Victorian and Edwardian times and sold very cheaply; one I obtained had a yellow label saying 37s 6d. on the back. But, like all things, they have their day. I note that the 1980 Lyle's antiques price guide lists them at £60. Maybe the Americans are buying them back again. Frankly, I think they're far more suited to Kentucky than South Kensington.

The three Bentwood chairs were interesting, and cheap enough at the time I bought them, goodness knows, at 50p each. I have seen them recently at as many pounds in trendy furnishing establishments specialising in stripped pine and microwave cookers. Bentwood was introduced into Austria in the mid-nineteenth century, and consisted of round strips of beech wood which, as the name suggests, were steamed and then bent into shape. No doubt you have sat on a few yourself in your village hall or tearooms. This familiar type of chair, very light, surprisingly strong and with a pierced plywood seat, is of course

16

still not worth a great deal; but find yourself a Bentwood rocking chair with elaborate scrolled legs and, if it is in good condition – and likely it will be – the price is near the £100 mark.

The 'pewter' tea service acquired for 90p turned out to be Britannia metal. This was a bit of a blow, but not too disastrous at less than £1. Britannia metal looks like pewter but is often shinier: this was hard to detect in the dark corners of Moses' hut. Pewter is an alloy of tin, lead and copper. Britannia metal is also an alloy – of tin, copper and antimony – and was invented during the mid-eighteenth century, when it was mass produced by a spinning process. It reached its heyday during Victoria's reign, when the name was patented by Richard Sturges. Early pieces were marked with an X surmounted by a crown; after 1840 they bear the legend EPBM, which stands for 'electroplated Britannia metal'. So long as you do not pay pewter prices for them, Britannia pieces in good condition are worth having. But avoid damaged articles – they are not worth the cost of repair.

The box of old 78 records I've still got. I've acquired others along the way, including a nice collection of early Ted Heath, Al Martino, Billy Eckstine and other crooners and big bands of the 1950s that feed my nostalgic memories of girls with pony tails and Ronnie Verrell drum solos at the Watford Odeon on a Sunday night. But it was not purely for nostalgic reasons that I kept them. I've suspected for some time that there's a whole sub-culture of old-record collectors who dress in 1950s macs and haunt the stalls of London street markets; when they're drunk they no doubt stagger round in circles at 78rpm! I reckon first-issue copies (and how do you *tell* a first issue?) of Glenn Miller, Fats Waller and Geraldo, among others, are worth good money. Try as I might, though, I have never found out how much, nor what the true collectors really want or where to find it. Nevertheless, it's a collecting field well worth exploring.

I also wish I had kept the old sewing machine. I let it go for a couple of pounds to a neighbour who wanted to run up a few baby's clothes. Then there was a wind-up gramophone of the 1930s that I bought at Moses' some weeks later, for which a friend rather reluctantly gave me £3. Seeing that Sotheby's are now taking an interest in mechanical items of the Twenties and Thirties, I wouldn't be in the least reluctant to offer my friends and neighbours a profit to buy back the unconsidered trifles from that Tuesday morning down 'The Tatty'.

Agreed, at the time there was nothing to set Bond Street alight, but not a bad morning's buying for £81.50. And remember, this wasn't the Middle Ages but just a few short years ago when, in Mr Moses' little hut and long before the world went mad, there was bread and butter *and* jam for anyone with a Tuesday morning to while away in a Kentish country market.

So having, almost by default, become some kind of dealer, I had to devise a means of selling all the goods that were filling my garage and spare rooms. I decided to open up shop at home. I was living at the time in a cottage that nestled on the edge of some very beautiful woods, in a country lane leading to an historic seaside village. It seemed an ideal spot to put up a board saying 'Antiques for Sale' in the hope that passing holidaymakers would pull in and browse round the rooms, making a selection from my bargains.

I bought an antique donkey cart, somehow got it home in the back of my Transit van, and stood it on the grass verge outside the gate with an old metal trunk on the top and a board in antique lettering advertising my curiosities. The china and furniture were arranged round the rooms of the cottage, looking for all the world as if I had lived with them for years, although some were in and out of there within twenty-four hours of purchase. The donkey cart and the idyllic setting did the trick, and soon cars could be heard reversing back up the lane for their occupants to satisfy their curiosity about what treasures might be awaiting them in this little cottage in the woods.

Most of our visitors liked to admire the cottage rather than what was in it, and when I was able to tell them that it was once owned by Noël Coward (actually his housekeeper lived in it) I was guaranteed rapt attention for at least twenty minutes. I used to add a tit-bit about the small horde of golden sovereigns that was found under the garage floor (once a barn) in the early 1960s, and the fact that it used to be a smuggler's cottage, and my visitors' captivation was complete. The trouble was, they were treating the place like a museum rather than a place of business. Most of them seemed to feel obliged to buy something, having taken up most of my morning, and I could see them furtively looking at prices as the time came to go, in the hope that they could find something for about 50p and make their escape. There were plenty of things in this price range, so a steady stream of day trippers went home happily clutching a knick-knack or two and saying that if I ever wanted to sell the cottage, please to let them know and here was their address.

All this was fine for my ego but did little for my bank balance. But then one day a rather smartly dressed chap arrived in a business-like manner and asked if he could look round. I was stripping a set of Victorian kitchen chairs in the garden at the time and my hands were covered in green paint and Nitromors blisters. But the prospect seemed sufficient to warrant cleaning up for fifteen minutes or so and I dipped my hands in a bucket of cold water and wiped myself down with some old curtains. My visitor was by this time well into dismantling a grandfather clock in the hall. It was only a 30-hour, he said, but he might be able to sell it if my price was right. I told him £45 and he pursed his lips and said he would think about it. I had heard that one before. Anyway, he put the clock together again and moved on into the lounge. Here, another clock attracted his attention. It was a rather attractive French brass mantel clock of about 1890 for which I was asking £95; I had bought it from a dealer friend for £65.

'No, it's only a cheap movement,' he said. 'That's too dear by half for me.'

I didn't let on, but I felt I might have made a big mistake in paying so much. As you will learn later, I was to wish I had never bought it at any price.

But my visitor passed on to other things and after a brief examination of each item he asked the trade price. It seemed he had a shop in one of the Cinque Ports and had seen my sign on his way back there.

Now, I had never actually been asked trade prices before, and although I now know it is customary to give other dealers about 10 per cent discount, I was letting this chap have pounds off, so keen was I to have a good sale. He was obviously doing quite nicely out of me because he bought one item in every three that I showed him. He had three sets of old brass carriage lamps I had bought from someone with an old barn and spent many hours

19

cleaning until they shone like new; £15 a pair I think he paid. He had a set of four Victorian dining chairs, some mahogany corner cupboards, a few bits and pieces of china, a marquetry stationery box; and, oh yes, he had the grandfather clock. He spent about £180 and, as I helped him load his car, he said he would make me a regular call on his buying round.

I was over the moon when he had gone. This was by far my biggest sale and I could really convince myself that I had 'arrived' in the antiques business. This sort of deal would make it all worthwhile. In fact this was my first real trade buyer and it taught me a strange fact about the antiques business which must make it unique in the world of commerce. It is the trade buyers that almost every antique dealer wants to patronise his business, not the public. At any given moment there are thousands of items of collectables passing on from dealer to dealer, who each add a small percentage to the price they paid and pass the goods on to their regular trade buyers. Nine times out of ten the public never get a sniff at any of them.

It is a good system, though, as it guarantees turnover and a small profit. The public makes very few purchases of antiques from the average antique shop: for lack of the money, the interest or the desire for such things. There are, of course, quite a few collectors around who prove the exception to this, but not nearly enough to keep Britain's antique dealers in business. So the main way of making a living, particularly in the rural areas, is to sell to other dealers who in turn have dealers who will buy certain items from them or who have private collectors for special pieces. There is a pecking order in all this, of course, and the man who sets the ball rolling has to be an expert in buying right so that the goods can be sent on their way as cheaply as possible to start with.

Usually antiques are bought first from a private vendor who does not know their true value or who has a house full of goods to get rid of and consequently calls in one of the house-clearance brigade. The house-clearer makes a bid for the lot, wardrobes and all, and obtains the choice bits as well, all at a knock-down price. The cups and saucers and all the modern stuff from Woolworths he sells off in back-street shops in the cheaper parts of the town where he operates, but all the good stuff goes straight out to his regular trade buyers at a competitive price, but at the same time making him a handsome profit. The knick-knacks in the house-clearers' little shops are usually acquired for nothing, so that's all profit as well. You would be amazed at how little some of these people pay for granny's old things when she dies: a houseful for £20 is by no means uncommon. Such deals are becoming harder to get now, of course, because TV and the Press are on the antiques bandwagon themselves at the moment and the general public is becoming a bit more knowledgeable about old things. The house-clearers still make a good living, none the less.

The other way to buy cheaply from the public is to go 'on the knocker', as they say. The technique here is to knock on the door of a likely looking house. (And if you don't want yours to be a likely looking house, don't leave Chinese vases in the window or have a nice faded mahogany card table on view in the sitting room for all to see as they pass along the pavement.) The 'knocker' will ask the householder if she has any old junk for sale. She will usually protest that she has none, but by the time she has said that the chap is in and admiring an old pot on her hall table.

'That's a very fine early Bellarmine water jar,' he tells the bewildered householder, who is currently keeping some plastic daffodils in it and was thinking of giving it to the dustman next week.

'Is it worth anything, then?' she asks.

'I'm not an authority on such things, madam,' he replies, 'but I should think I could let you have about £200 for it. I'd need to let my friend have a look at it. He's an expert on such things. I could get him to come round tomorrow night, if that's convenient.'

The householder, flustered and not quite believing her luck, says yes that would be quite all right, and a thought flashes through her mind that she wished she hadn't thrown into the dustbin the other five Bellarmine jars she had from her mother; still, £200 for this one would be rather nice.

By now the 'knocker' is on into the living room and the lady of the house has the adrenalin flowing and is beginning to think it's her birthday.

'Now, madam, you might just have a few more things you didn't know the value of.'

He expertly goes round the room, lifting up a vase here and getting under a table there. He does this all round the house, breezily going from room to room, his computer-like mind assessing exactly what he wants, how much he will pay and how much he will get for it.

'Well, there's no more Bellarmine pots or anything, madam,' he says. 'But I might be able to give you a few pounds for that old desk in the dining room' (actually, a rather nice Georgian mahogany bureau on bracket feet with the original brass drop handles). 'I could clear it for you for £25. And those vases with funny looking birds on them in the front room, I could go to £10 for them if you're interested; oh, and £15 for the old card table in the lounge. That would make quite a nice little sum for you with the £200 for the Bellarmine jar.'

Ah, yes, the Bellarmine jar. The lady has already mentally spent the money for that on new curtains and a three-piece suite.

'Yes, I suppose that's all right,' she says. 'When will you come for the jar?'

'Well if it's OK with you, lady, I'll give you the £50 cash now for the odds and ends I'm having, and I'll come round with my friend George and the £200 for the jar tomorrow evening. I'd just like him to check it before I spend so much money. But he'll certainly have it from you . . . may even give you a bit more than that for it.'

The lady, beaming now, helps our friend load the 'bits and pieces' into his van, and off he goes. And for £50 he has acquired a good bureau, an excellent pair of First Period Worcester blue scale vases and a more than useful Regency card table. One thousand pounds worth of goods for fifty quid. Not a bad morning's business. The lady, by the way, is still waiting for 'George' to turn up. But 'George' won't be coming. Even if he exists, he is certainly not interested in paying £200 for a Doulton & Lambeth harvest jug, circa 1900!

So that is another way the unscrupulous end of the trade start the goods off on their travels at rock-bottom prices.

Of course, not all dealers are like that and the great majority of them pay fair prices to the public for everything they buy.

They leave themselves a reasonable profit, but that is business and no one would begrudge them that. And thankfully the aforementioned publicity is numbering the days of the almost criminal section of the trade.

I didn't find all this out overnight, of course. But it was that dealer who visited my little cottage in the woods who set me out on the complex road to antique dealing. He gave me a good sale that summer morning and indirectly was the cause of all the subsequent pleasures and adventures I had in the fascinating world of antiques. Some of these are told in the remaining chapters of this book.

2
Goss and a World Record

I first became aware of Goss china when a friend of mine, Robert, who was then running an antiques and bric-à-brac shop, showed me a small and rather quaint piece of white china in the form of a kettle; on the base was a logo of a falcon and the words W. H. GOSS in capital letters underneath. The Worcester coat of arms was on the side.

'If you get any of these I'll pay you £1 a lump for them,' he said. 'Cottages and bigger bits fetch £5 up,' he added.

Little did I realise that the hunt for what I considered then to be practically worthless seaside souvenirs was to lead to one of my biggest thrills in the world of antiques.

William Henry Goss learnt the art of potting from the famous Copeland firm, one of the biggest factories in the Stoke Potteries. Details of the early part of Goss's career are uncertain but it is known that he had his own company in London Road, Stoke, in 1870. This was to become known as the Falcon Works – hence the falcon in the mark I was shown by Robert. William's son, Adolphus, joined the firm as a manager in the early 1880s and it was his influence that saw the manufacture of the little models which I thought of as gifts from the seaside.

All sorts of little models were produced in white-glazed parian ware. They were usually copies of items of historical interest, such as a Bath Roman Ewer, a model of a Roman ewer found in that city and to be seen in Dorset Museum. Another model was that of a Canterbury Leather Bottle, a model of the 'Pilgrim leather bottell' in Canterbury Museum. Well over 300 items such as these were made before the Goss factory went into decline in the 1920s, and was eventually sold to the firm of George Jones & Sons Ltd in 1929. Jones themselves collapsed in the mid-1930s, when the Goss name was acquired by Cauldron Potteries. No Goss models were made after 1940, although the trade mark is now owned by the Coalport Group.

As well as the aforementioned miscellany of models, very few of which stand much over 100mm high, Goss made miniature items of footwear, like a model of Queen Victoria's first shoe; fonts, as in the model of the font in which Shakespeare was baptised; lighthouses; animals; crosses, such as Banbury Cross; models of monuments like the Cenotaph in Whitehall; and, probably the most sought-after of all, a range of cottages, the first three ever made by the firm being Anne Hathaway's, Robert Burns's and Shakespeare's cottages. Altogether, there are just short of 500 known models of all types made by W. H. Goss.

Hop Kiln   Headcorn

Wordsworth's House

Priest's House
Prestbury

Burns' Cottage

Abbot's Kitchen , Glastonbury

Bunyan's Cottage
Elstow

Shakespeare's House

On seeing my first Goss model I must admit that, although I conceded it had a certain quaint appeal, it wasn't my idea of antique porcelain, nor could I imagine collecting it myself. But that was what the trade wanted and I had to earn a living: so the hunt was on.

I soon began to pick up a piece here and there, often on market stalls and occasionally by courtesy of Mr Moses down 'The Tatty'. Eventually I had seven or eight pieces, mainly uninspiring little things like jugs, ewers and vases. I took them all in a box along to Robert and, sure enough, although I'd paid as little as 10p each for some of them, £1 a lump is what he gave for them. I think the retail price in his shop was £1.50 to £2 each – so both of us made some money, which was how, as I was fast learning, the trade worked.

Before long Goss-hunting became something of an obsession with me. I even began to like the stuff, but it was some months before I personally came across Goss cottages. Even then I would not have recognised them except that the shop where I saw them had a notice saying 'Cottages like these marked W. H. Goss bought for cash'. I had not been able to find any literature on the subject, so I was rather surprised to note that these rather drab unglazed models were related to the much brighter Goss items I had been used to handling. However, there they were in the window and I was able to get a close look at what Robert and others would pay me £5 a lump for.

Not long after this I went, as I usually did, to the monthly auction of Hatch and Waterman at Tenterden, where I would sit all day in the hot and dusty high-roofed saleroom buying anything that I thought would make me a pound or two. There were always 600 lots or more which were skilfully sold in about six hours by Pauline Chalk, one of the few lady auctioneers in the country and a partner in the firm. Mrs Chalk knew all the techniques of the trade but, with such a vast amount of stuff to get through on sale days, not surprisingly a few things always crept through cheaply. The first and last fifty lots were where the bargains lay, for either the bidders were still too sleepy to raise their eyebrows or else, at the end of the day, they were too tired to take any interest.

But the lot I had set my mind on this particular day was

somewhere around 120 – a box of crested china. I had seen it on view day where some other dealer had hidden it under the rostrum. This had immediately made me suspect there was something good in it. Sure enough, in a cardboard box originally designed for Rowntree's Kit-Kat bars nestled thirty-two Goss pieces, including rarities like a World War I tank, a tea service, a lobster trap bearing the arms of Abingdon, an armorial teapot stand, a rather odd-looking piece which turned out to be a model of a Kentish hopkiln at Headcorn ... and a model of Burns's cottage. Kit-Kat bars could never be sweeter than this little lot!

On the day of the sale I positioned myself nice and early in a seat in the middle of the saleroom dead opposite the seeking eyes of Mrs Chalk. On my left was a fat woman with a flask of coffee, which she drank noisily, and a bag of biscuits of the crunchy ginger kind, the consuming of which broke the lull between lots like machine-gun fire. If she was a nuisance then, she was to be an absolute menace when 'Lot 120: A box of crested miniatures' came up. Trust me to pick the wrong seat!

Anyway, I was determined to have this box of Goss and had mentally decided to pay £32 for it – the stipulated £1 a lump. I was such a tyro that I could not imagine selling again at a profit should this magic figure be exceeded.

I smoked two cigarettes between Lots 100 and 119, but still had enough voice left to open the bidding for Lot 120 at £5. There was a pause of indifference which made me think I was going to be a maiden bidder, when another maiden, in the form of the fat woman next to me, made a jump bid – to £10. I could see I was in for trouble.

'Looking for £12.50,' said Mrs Chalk.

I nodded.

'Fifteen, Mrs Humphreys?' (The woman was a friend of the auctioneer's!) 'Yes, fifteen I have.'

I nodded again for £17.50 and then a fresh bidder came in at £20. It was an artful dodger I knew from 'The Tatty' who more than likely had hidden the box behind the rostrum on view day.

Mrs Chalk played the artful dodger off against Mrs Humphreys all the way up to £30 and, on asking for £32.50, caught my nod. The fat woman and the artful dodger remained silent and the auctioneer began the countdown.

'Going once, going twice,' said Mrs Chalk. Then her gavel fell to conclude the deal. They were mine!

'Name, please,' asked the auctioneer.

The words 'Humphreys' and 'Austen' came out simultaneously. The fat woman and I glared at one another.

'You didn't bid again, Mrs Humphreys; I sold them to the gentleman on your right,' said Mrs Chalk.

'I called out £32.50,' said the fat woman, spluttering her gingernut crumbs.

'I'm sorry, I didn't take you, Mrs Humphreys. Is there a dispute; shall I put them up again?'

'Yes, please,' said Mrs Humphreys, 'I'll start you off at £20.'

'Twenty-two pounds, Mr Austen?' Mrs Chalk looked at me. I nodded. I was furious. This aggressive coffee-swiller was obviously determined to have them. I began mentally preparing to go to £50 to make sure she didn't.

The artful dodger came in again with a nuisance bid at £28, but didn't say anything when Mrs Humphreys said a firm 'yes' at £30.

I gave an even firmer nod at £32 (Mrs Chalk had dispensed with the pences this time). I saw the fat woman start to say something when asked for £2 more, but just as she did so a crumb must have caught in her throat, for she gave a horrific, face-reddening cough and waved her hand in a swishing motion across the front of her face as Mrs Chalk repeated her request. Mrs Humphreys was too convulsed with choking to take any further part in the proceedings and, as she groped in her carrier bag for a flask of coffee to swill away the irritant crumb, the lot was again knocked down to me – at £32. Yes, £1 a lump! Mrs Humphreys was led from the saleroom by her diminutive male companion, who patted her back all the way to the door, and I heaved a sigh of relief for the crumb of comfort I had obtained from the fat woman's gingernuts. Goodness knows how much she might have gone on to pay had her insatiable appetite not got the better of her.

I was able to clear my purchases before the end of the sale, so I beat a hasty retreat back home, where I celebrated my day's dealing with a cup of tea, with which I declined to take biscuits!

Checking through the box of Goss at leisure, I was pleased to find the lot had proved a very good buy indeed. There was a model of Burns's cottage, about 2½in long, a British tank with the Arms of Faversham, a Jersey fish basket, a pot modelled like a limpet, an armorial teapot stand, various other models of rather less character, and another cottage-type model impressed underneath, 'Hop Kiln, Headcorn, Kent.' It had terracotta brickwork, a slate-grey roof and pale-brown ventilator and was unglazed. Rather nondescript, I thought.

I decided to put the better models up for sale in my cottage, and sell twenty-five or so of the run-of-the-mill items to Robert for £1 each. The tank I priced at £5, Burns's cottage at £8, the teapot stand at £3.50 and the hop kiln at £7. I put them on display in the china cabinet and hoped they would soon find an eager collector ready to pay what I thought were rather high prices.

A strange thing when you are dealing in antiques is that you seem to get runs of the same kind of goods. I once had three bureaux in stock the same week, four longcase clocks, seven corner cupboards, and so on. There seems to be no reason for this, but it has happened too often to ignore it.

And so it proved to be with the Goss. The sale had been on the Thursday, and the next day I bought the local newspaper as I always did, intent on finding any goodies for sale in the classified advertisement columns. Before I had scanned many column inches I came across the following entry:

'Collector willing to sell large collection of Goss china. Various prices. Benenden'.

By now I was beginning to feel a bit of an expert in the stuff, so I phoned up immediately and asked what there was for sale. It appeared there were something like eighty different Goss pieces for disposal at an average price of £3 each. I protested that they seemed a bit dear for me to make any profit, but I agreed to go out to Benenden that evening to have a look. I thought that either I could beat the vendor down or else there might be some other stuff available to buy which he didn't think very much of.

So off I went into the Kentish summer evening and along the lanes to Benenden. I eventually found the isolated detached house surrounded by tall trees along a quiet country track. On being ushered into the lounge by the owner and collector of Goss china, I was immediately confronted with an enormous table spread with umpteen items of Goss – ewers, Roman urns, pots, cups and saucers, lobster pots and so on. All were meticulously priced with individual labels, and the owner and his wife sat primly in their chairs, unsmiling and with rather hard-looking faces. I could see I was unlikely to get any bargains here.

But I conscientiously got down to examining each model individually, trying to make polite conversation as I did so. 'That's an interesting one' . . . 'Haven't seen that before' . . . , and other remarks. All the time I knew the prices asked were way above what I could pay for what were rather ordinary pieces of Goss.

As a further gambit I asked if they had any of the Goss cottage models, as I would be more interested in them than in the pieces on display, of which I had rather a lot in stock.

'Yes, we've got most of the cottages,' said Mr Grim. 'But they're not for sale. These are our duplicates which we're prepared to dispose of,' he added rather pompously.

'Any chance of seeing them?' I asked, reluctant to see a wasted trip.

Mr Grim looked at his wife and, receiving a nod of assent, went to a corner cupboard and proceeded to produce a stream of cottages and busts, most of which I had never before associated with Mr Goss. This was all broadening my education and I was able to see more models than one would normally encounter in many years. They were obviously worth a great deal of money.

'We're almost complete on the cottages,' said Mr Grim. 'There's only one we'll probably never stand a chance of getting. It's the rarest of all the Goss pieces. A book on the subject I own says there were only three models made of the Headcorn hop kiln.'

'Hop kiln?' I queried. 'What does it look like?'

'Nothing special,' said Mr Grim. 'Less than two or three inches high and unglazed, painted in dull colours. Got "Hop Kiln, Headcorn, Kent" impressed on the base. Of course, I've never seen one, I'm just going by the description in the book.'

'Do you think I could see the book?' I asked, a flush of adrenalin beginning to run through me.

A tome on Goss china written by Messrs Rees and Cawley was produced from the bookshelf. As I remember, there were only two or three lines about the hop kiln, but the book really did say that only three were known and that it was the rarest of the Goss cottages.

'You're not going to believe this,' I said, trying to conceal a growing sense of excitement. 'I've got that model myself.'

'Oh have you,' said Mr Grim, rather flatly. 'Very lucky. Where did you get it?'

I told them the story of the lucky buy in the saleroom the day before and they could hardly believe it. Benenden was only 10 miles from Tenterden and from under their noses had been snatched the one model Mr and Mrs Grim would have given their eye-teeth to own.

They rarely went to that auction, they said, and had no idea there was any Goss for sale – which was just as well for me because, with their knowledge of the rarity of the hop kiln, I would have stood no chance of buying it.

After I had described mine to them in detail the couple had absolutely no doubt that I had the real McCoy. They were congratulatory but the atmosphere seemed tinged with a little bitterness that the tyro had received such bountiful luck.

I was so elevated by my discovery that I cannot recall much of what passed during the rest of the evening. I seem to remember paying over-priced amounts for a half-dozen or so pieces, as much in gratitude for the information as anything else, and then driving home hell for leather to rescue the hop kiln from the china cabinet before someone snapped it up for the £7 I was asking. I had a dreadful feeling that a customer might have called at the cottage that evening and bought it.

But no, it was really my day: all the models were still there. I removed the hop kiln, Burns's cottage, the tank and one or two other items from display and went to bed dreaming of what the hop kiln might be worth to a Goss collector . . . £30 or £40 at least, I imagined.

Robert bought the lesser items from me at the agreed price and was fascinated to see the hop kiln, of which he had not heard. He found it hard to believe there were only three of them known and said he wouldn't like to guess what it might be worth.

I brooded over the matter for a week or two, deciding the best way to dispose of it for the highest price. In the end, hearing that an antique dealer friend, Ivy Atkinson from Canterbury, was going to take some dolls for sale at Sotheby's, Belgravia, I offered to drive her there and take my better Goss pieces along with me. Probably they would turn their noses up, but it was worth a try.

The enormous publicity obtained by Sotheby's and the other major London auction houses ensures a constant stream of hopefuls through their doors, clutching their treasures in the hope that they have an undiscovered masterpiece which will make them rich beyond their wildest dreams. I don't think Ivy and I imagined we were about to become wealthy but we nevertheless had hope in our hearts as we joined the little queue that dealt with our particular specialism.

In front of us, old ladies with turn-of-the-century pottery and hairstyles to match were being rather peremptorily turned away with comments like, 'It's very modern, madam. Probably around 1910. Dalton. Not very attractive and I suggest you put it in your local auction. It's worth about £8.' And in those few words a whole day, if not a lifetime, was obviously ruined for someone who had maybe train-journeyed from Chichester with a family heirloom, only to discover it was worth less than the cost of the rail ticket. I suppose the experts behind the counter saw instances of this all day and every day and had no energy left to soften the blow or offer platitudes of sympathy.

Soon it was our turn to face the experts. Ivy's dolls came first. She held out a superb Hoffmeister porcelain doll, dressed in original clothes and in perfect condition.

'I'm wondering what you think of this,' said Ivy.

'It's nineteenth-century, quite late, Hoffmeister.'

'Yes, I know the date and maker,' said Ivy. 'What I want to know is how much you think it would fetch in your sale.'

'Oh, we wouldn't handle it, madam. It's worth only about £10.'

'Ten pounds!' shrieked Ivy. 'But I paid over £100 for it, young man, and I can get nearly £200 for it in the shop.'

'Well, I wish you every success, madam,' replied Old Etonian. 'We couldn't get anything like that for it here.'

'How much *could* you get for it, then?' asked Ivy.

32

'About £60, I should think,' said Old Etonian, who seemed impatient to be away for afternoon tea and toast.

I began to wonder what kind of game this was. Was it worth £10 or was it worth £60? It seemed to me it could be worth £1,000 for all this expert knew. Eventually Ivy beat him up to a £150 reserve and both parties seemed quite happy. What an amazing game! Ivy left a number of other dolls, plus a Celadon plate and some other Oriental items, after much haggling over reserves.

Now it was my turn.

'Oh, Goss is it,' said Old Etonian. 'I don't deal with that sort of stuff. I'll get our specialist.'

The chap duly arrived and thankfully turned out to be an enthusiastic, obviously knowledgeable young man who was genuinely taken aback to see the 'Hop Kiln, Headcorn, Kent' which I produced from my bag.

'I'm told there are only three of these models known,' I said.

'I believe you're right,' said Mr Enthusiast. 'I'll get Rees and Cawley and look it up.'

Rees and Cawley was obviously the Goss collector's bible.

'Yes, here we are: only three models known. Quite right, sir. Well, that's most interesting; it's the first one I've seen. We'd be happy to put that in our next Goss specialist sale in the autumn, if you'd like.'

I was more than happy to agree, and then asked the delicate but crucial question about price.

'I should think £200 to £300, sir. Depends who's there. I would recommend a reserve price of £180, if that's acceptable.'

Acceptable! I should say it was. The whole thing seemed quite incredible. This nondescript item picked up on the cheap in a country auction was worth all that? Perhaps those big-money antiques stories were true after all.

It seemed I was to find out on the last day of October, a Thursday, for that was the date fixed for the sale. A few weeks after my visit to Sotheby's their sale catalogue arrived, with eight lots of mine listed under the Goss section. Lot 104 was the Hop Kiln, Headcorn, Kent, described as 'a very rare model . . . Rees and Cawley record this as the rarest of the series of cottages with only three examples known to them'. There was a photograph of it, too, although I had to admit that the model looked anything but exciting and I could not imagine anyone wanting to spend £180 on such a thing.

I determined to attend the sale, regardless of what it would do for my migraine! So I set off early on the main line to Charing Cross and dreamt my way across the West End to Belgravia. The sale was due to start at 10.30 am, but by 9.55 the room was crowded with potential bidders having a final preview. No one seemed particularly interested in anything of mine. I watched closely, and although a couple of people had a cursory look at the hop kiln and Burns's Cottage, main interest seemed to be in Staffordshire commemorative wares, which were also on offer that day.

There were a lot of pot lids, too. I dare say that those gentlemen who, during the early days of the nineteenth century, were in their dressing-rooms smearing bears' grease on their hair while their good ladies were downstairs instructing their servants about which fish paste to put in the afternoon-tea sandwiches, would have expressed great surprise that the lids to the pots in which these products were sold were to attract interest in auction rooms. But that was how pot lids decorated with quaint little pictures of bears in humanised form, pursuing such activities as going to school or reading newspapers, started life. Bears' grease was a popular hair dressing at the time, so what more natural than that bears should appear on the lids of the pots in which it was sold. Similarly with potted shrimps, meats, fish pastes, etc: lids were decorated with scenes of Pegwell Bay in Kent where the shrimps were caught. Throughout the rest of the century a multitude of different motifs appeared, depicting a range of designs from famous stately homes, through scenes from Shakespeare to sports and pastimes. The Staffordshire firm of F. & R. Pratt & Co of Fenton made most of these lids. Around 1845 they discovered a method of cheap underglaze printing in colour, and for the next fifty years or so their colourful lids appeared on a variety of products. And the comparatively few of those lids which have survived to the present in perfect condition are now highly regarded as collectors' items, with several hundreds of pounds being paid for the rare and early lids with the bear motifs. As I was interested in pot lids myself, I had a good look at them all, and made a few notes in the catalogue about prices I would pay if I had a chance. But as this was Sotheby's I hardly expected to be in the running.

At 10.30 prompt the porters ushered viewers to their seats and the auctioneer bustled efficiently into the room, immaculately dressed and with just a trace of after-shave. It was Mr Enthusiast himself, the expert who had taken my Goss in over the counter.

The pot lids were sold first, the bidding going like a dose of salts — far quicker than I had experienced in country auction rooms, where the auctioneers often spent as much time talking about the weather or cracking feeble jokes as they did in actually selling the stuff. In the event the pot lid prices were surprisingly low: French Street Scene and Dr Johnson went for £14 each; the Late Prince Consort and On Guard both fetched £10. All these lids I could have sold in local country auctions for £25 each, no trouble at all, but somehow I could not bring myself to give the auctioneer a nod. Maybe it was first-visit-to-Sotheby's nerves or, more likely, that I couldn't think of much else other than the Headcorn Hop Kiln.

I sat through the commemoratives, and then Lot 94, Burns's Cottage, arrived next to the rostrum. I had reserved it at £20 and was a bit dismayed when the bidding was started at a fiver. But not to worry, the auctioneer soon knocked it down for a satisfactory £26.

The rest of the cottages made good money, the rare model of a Goss oven eventually fetching £200. After it came Lot 104, the hop kiln. The porter who brought it to the rostrum almost totally hid it in his large hand before rather quizzically holding it up to the gathering. One man at the front removed his glasses and peered forward for a closer look, but other than that the room was still as the auctioneer asked if anyone would start at £100. Nobody would, so he started it himself at £50, much to the astonishment of the aforementioned porter, who did a double take at the kiln and seemed to grasp it rather more firmly now he realised it was such an estimable property.

The bidding went quite firmly to £150 in very little time; it then dithered a bit until it settled on £195. It could be sold for that, of course, as the reserve was £180. It seemed nobody would top it up to £200. The auctioneer tried his hardest to get more but it appeared the bidder in the centre of the room was to be lucky. I sensed it was about to be knocked down when, with a flurry of fluttering catalogue pages, a lady in glasses in the front of the room bid the magical £200. The centre-room bidder was shocked to be asked for a £25 jump, but the auctioneer got it, plus an immediate response at £250 from catalogue-waver. Then the battle was joined as, in £25 jumps, two ardent Goss collectors joined battle in Belgravia until, with a final triumphant flourish of her catalogue, the lady in the front row said 'yes' at £500 and the hop kiln was hers. She deserved it.

I remember little about the rest of the sale. I did at least manage to note the prices obtained by the rest of my lots, for profit estimates later, but not even the fresh air in Motcomb Street afterwards could sober my feeling of elation as I headed back home.

A few days later I received a letter from Derek Chapman, General Manager of Sotheby's Belgravia, saying 'I do hope you were pleased with the price obtained for the Oast House. A new world record, I am told, for a Goss cottage.' I think I was more pleased about that record than the cheque for £673 which was also enclosed. Not a bad profit on an outlay of £32.

There is a strange twist to the tale of the Headcorn Hop Kiln. A week or two later I was chatting in Ivy's antique shop with another dealer, who happened to drop in. Ivy introduced us, then said, much to my surprise: 'Peter, Tony here says it was *his* hop kiln Sotheby's sold last month.'

'*Yours?*' I asked him incredulously. 'I can assure you it was very definitely mine. I bought it in a Tenterden sale some time ago.'

'Maybe you did,' he said, in a rather cocky way I didn't much take to. 'But it so happens I had a hop kiln as well. I bought it from old lady in Margate. I sent it to Sotheby's in September and I hear on the grapevine it fetched £500 in the October sale.'

'What did it look like?' I asked, desperate for something to say to counteract the sinking feeling in my stomach. He described it accurately enough and I nodded my head and said, 'Well, it's just a fantastic coincidence. But I can assure you it wasn't your model they sold last month. If you delivered it in September it was a good month after they had mine, and as they had mine first they'd have sold mine first. And anyway, I've got the money and cashed the cheque,' I added defiantly, just managing to control an urge to stamp my foot. 'No doubt yours will come up in due course.'

He was still adamant it was his hop kiln that broke the world record. But I knew it wasn't.

* * * * * * * *

Even that isn't the end of my good fortune with Goss. A year or two later, staying in a New Forest hotel where a local dealer put a few pieces of china up for sale in a cabinet in the residents' dining room, my wife, Joy, picked up a white parian bust labelled Copeland and priced £3.50. Encouraging me to buy it, she waited for the deal to be concluded before leading me back to the dining table, pouring me another cup of coffee and then, with a knowing smile, turning the item over and saying, 'I think that says Goss, don't you?'

And sure enough, my wife had spotted, almost imperceptibly inscribed in the underside of the model, the signature 'W. H. Goss' scrawled in the paste with, nearby, the trade mark. Unless you held the bust at a certain angle, you could see nothing at all. That is why the dealer had thought the word 'Copeland' was as good as any other label to stick on it and £3.50 a fair enough price. But Joy, who has helped me find a few other bargains in her time, was instrumental in spotting a rare early piece of Goss, signed by the potter himself. It still lies in one of my bottom drawers, although I have yet to identify whom it represents. It would be nice to think we shall break another world record with it one day . . . .

3

The Wild Man of Romney Marsh

Dealing in antiques requires one to keep a list of 'prospects' in much the same way as a life assurance salesman – except that my 'prospects' were people I could *buy* from rather than *sell* to. I never found it difficult to sell anything I had in stock. The real problem was in acquiring goods at the right price. I thus always had my ears attuned to the local jungle drums in the hope of hearing a beat that would say there were antiques for sale. And it was in the course of following up one of my leads that I encountered the Wild Man of Romney Marsh.

Old Henry, a retired local farmer, used to call in at a hostelry not far from my home to buy a pint or two of that most potent of Kentish local brews – Bob Luck's cider. And it was in the bar of the White Horse that I first got talking to Henry, a tall and friendly man of around seventy years who despite a permanent stoop, due to years of hay stacking and loading corn waggons, was still over 6ft 3in tall. His giant hands were permanently curved with arthritis, but the shape was convenient for holding pint mugs, so Henry had no trouble at all in enjoying himself propped on a stool in the public bar.

I remember my initial conversation with him about the old horse brasses around the pub fireplace. One thing led to another, so that when he heard of my interest in antiques he invited me to his bungalow to share a pint of Bob Luck's and have a look at his own extensive collection of brassware.

One Tuesday evening I found Henry's bungalow on Romney Marsh and hammered on the door. Always when I called there I was to hear the thunderous and long-drawn-out 'Cum Eeeeeen' from the back room, and always I would find the door unlocked and Henry hidden in a cloud of Lloyd's Skipper smoke in his neat sitting-room. His huge frame occupied most of a three-seater settee trimly upholstered in green stretch covers. After preliminary greetings Henry would shuffle to the kitchen for a flagon of cider and two cut-glass tumblers. His great red hands would shake as he poured the cider into our glasses and over the dining table but, although I once offered to pour, he seemed to think it would undermine his position as host not to dispense the drinks, so I respected his wish and simply helped him mop up the table afterwards.

On my first visit to Henry's I was indeed impressed with his room full of brass. There were candlesticks, goblins from Dartmoor, dustpans and brushes, brass mirrors, wall plaques, ashtrays and clocks, and — his pride and joy — a brass and copper electric fire dating from the 1930s. Dotted round the room were charming little items of Victorian furniture — tripod tables, a work-table, set of four balloon-back chairs, books, china and an enormous Victorian Gothic sideboard in mahogany.

Now any of this gear was highly saleable, so interspersed with my pleasantries with Henry were little feelers to assess whether, and for how much, he would part with any of it. I would, for example, talk about his work-table and Henry would ask me how

much it was worth. I would reply by inquiring how much did he want for it and he would insist I make an offer. Now the truth was that I was not really sure how much it was worth, so I used to end up saying I would see how much my customer would pay for it and come back next week and tell him. And that is what I did.

I would see one of my trade buyers and ask him how much he would give me for a small Victorian work-table in mahogany on tripod feet with original fittings. I would get an offer of, say, £65, and go back and offer Henry £30. And always he would say, 'I i'nt sellin' it.' It became a kind of game. But I was prepared to play because a) I enjoyed Henry's company; and b) I thought one day I would win.

Now in case you are thinking that Henry was the Wild Man of Romney Marsh I had better say at once that he wasn't. It was week three of my calls at Henry's bungalow that I encountered the real thing. On the Friday night Henry announced that Tom and Rosie would be popping over for a drink that evening. And at 8 pm precisely there was a shuffling of feet in the hall and a shortish, thick-set man, aged about forty-six, with wavy golden hair and a large wife stepped into the sitting-room. I was eyed suspiciously by both. I was not introduced, but after the cider had been poured we exchanged a few pleasantries and Tom said: 'I hear you do a bit of dealin', fellah.'

I admitted that I did and Tom said what he was after was Royal Crown Derby china. He would buy any I had and pay top money for it, as he already had one of the finest and rarest collections for many miles around.

Now, gipsy caravans are filled with the brightly coloured and richly gilt products of the Royal Crown Derby factory. Gipsies treasure it as highly as gold sovereigns and baked hedgehog. And although Tom lived in a council house the other side of the green, a close examination of his features revealed definite Romany extraction. The oily skin, sparkling dark eyes and thick wavy hair I could visualise over a woodsmoke fire in any lay-by in the county. And his taste for garish porcelain and brassware confirmed my theory. He also had a big and powerful car – a Rover 2000. 'There's nobody, neither police nor racing drivers, can catch me in that,' he once confided to me.

Tom was full of such boastful remarks, and indeed he had an

absurdly romantic view of his whole life-style. Everything he did was the cleverest, and everything he owned the biggest, the best, the rarest or most desirable. His large wife was certainly included in one of the above categories, and powerfully-built as Tom was, I strongly suspected that Rosie knocked him for six to conclude any domestic tiff *they* had. But of one boast Tom did not exaggerate, and that was of his collection of brassware, surpassing even Henry's.

I soon became chummy with Tom and Rosie and was invited to examine their treasures. After I had said 'hello' to grandad and the parrot in the kitchen I was ushered into the living-room, where Tom looked at me with wild, sparkling eyes and led me to the china cabinet. And there was shelf upon shelf bursting with so-called cigar-pattern Crown Derby – cups, saucers, plates and milk jugs, sugar bowls, eggcups and teapots.

Tom watched me examining it all, then said: 'Know how much that lot cost me, fellah?'

I hesitated, lest the price I quoted gave him too much idea of what it was *really* worth.

'Fifteen quid, fellah. Bought it from a woman in Ashford near where we had the road up.'

Tom, it seemed, dug trenches for the water board.

'Know how much it's worth, fellah?'

'I should think nearer £50,' I said, reasonably frankly.

'Five hundred pounds, fellah. That's what Rosie's insured it for – £500.'

I swallowed and nodded. 'Very wise,' I said. 'I'm sure it's worth every penny.' What I thought was: how absurd; they'd get about £80 for it in auction. No point in trying to buy any of this.

After I had examined the Crown Derby, my eye was taken by an enormous brass coffee pot of Turkish appearance decorated with typical Benares designs of three-legged deities and sacred animals.

'Know what that is, fellah?' asked Tom, his eyes positively rolling.

'Looks like a brass coffee pot,' I said sarcastically.

'That, fellah, is a Christian urn. Made 5,000 years before Christ, fellah.'

'It's probably priceless, then,' I said, even more sarcastically.

But the great thing with Tom was that he was so full of himself that he actually believed what you said.

'Money couldn't buy that,' said Tom. 'A chap I know at Newchurch dug that up near the church. I did him a small favour and he let me have it. It was probably in the church long before Christ was thought of,' added Tom, as if explaining its 'Christian' significance.

Tom's garbled knowledge of history was a constant, but secret, delight to me. Unbelievable as some of the things he said were, he none the less believed them and would mock you for *your* ignorance if you dared to take issue with him.

'Now look at these,' said Tom, leading me into another room. And there on countless shelves were enormous brass clocks in the shape of stags and cupids, barometers, a brass calendar, sets of fire irons, coal hods, vases and jugs. All were in brass and they glittered like gipsy gold in the firelight. The clocks alone were worth hundreds of pounds.

Dumbstruck, all I could say was: 'I've got a rather nice brass clock for sale myself. It was featured on *Going for a Song* (a BBC programme on antiques that was being televised at that time). Not the actual one *I've* got, you understand,' I said. 'But one like it. It's got a French movement and a Regency brass case. They said it was worth about £95,' I added.

'I'll buy that off you, fellah,' said Tom. 'How much do you want for it?'

'Well,' I hesitated, sensing a deal. 'I paid £65 for it, so I couldn't really let it go for less than £75.'

'I could probably go to thirty quid, fellah,' said Tom, eyes glinting and ignoring what I had said about my costs. He was obviously personally so used to spinning yarns about his transactions that he assumed I was tarred with the same brush and had probably bought it for 65p.

'But I paid £65 for it myself,' I said. 'I've got to take a profit on it.'

'Well, look here, fellah, I'll tell you what I'll do, I'll look out a few pounds worth of stuff I don't want and we'll do a deal. Bring it round to Henry's on Friday night and I'll tell you whether it's worth anything. Rosie gets paid on Fridays,' he added.

Tom obviously did not put much trust in Arthur Negus or

Going for a Song – a programme he had never heard of, incidentally, despite a 25in colour TV in the corner of his kitchen. I suppose the programme smacked of culture, or something.

So I agreed with his suggestion, on the basis that if I could wheedle some of his Crown Derby out of him, and maybe a lump or two of brass, I could do quite nicely out of it all.

Meantime, on the intervening Wednesday night, I called on Henry for a chat. Tom and Rosie were already there. After the cider ceremony, Henry said: 'Know anyone who wants to buy a sideboard?'

Stunned at this sign that they were actually willing to *sell* something, I said I would buy it, even though I knew it was a monstrous piece that only a shipping trade dealer would want. But I thought I could get it for £30.

'How much do you want for it, then?' I asked.

'Seven hundred pounds, fellah,' chipped in Tom with a complacent grin, from the depths of an armchair.

'That's ridiculous,' I protested. 'It's only Victorian, it's too big and it's worth only a tenth of that.'

'No, t'aint,' said Henry. 'What did the dealer say it was, Tom?'

'Gothic,' said Tom authoritatively.

'Yes, that's it,' said Henry. 'That carving on it's mediaeval.'

'But the whole shape of it's Victorian,' I protested. 'They didn't have looking-glasses on sideboards in mediaeval times.'

'They did 200 years ago,' said Tom.

'Yes,' I replied, 'but that wasn't the Middle Ages; that was Georgian.'

'Well, you're wrong, fellah,' said Tom, warming to the argument.

'Anyway, that's what I've sold it for,' said Henry, his normally impassive face gleeful.

'Well, if you've sold it, why are you offering it to me?' I asked.

'Cos he a'int coming for it till the weekend,' replied Henry.

I asked who this 'he' was.

'Had a dealer round this morning, didn't you, Henry.' It was Rosie joining in the oneupmanship now. 'Bought a lot of stuff, didn't he, Henry. Paid good money for it too.'

'He did, he did,' chuckled Henry.

43

My heart sank. I'd been pipped at the post. I asked what he had sold him.

'Tables, chairs, some of me brass, a tea service and some postcards,' said Henry.

'But I offered to buy those many times.'

'Yes, but you never put your money where your mouth was, fellah,' chipped in Tom.

'You never said how much you wanted,' I protested. 'I'd have paid good money for all that stuff. Anyhow, how much did you get for it?'

'He give me sixty quid for the sewing table, the tripod table and the set of four dining chairs, plus the other bits and pieces. Paid me cash, too, lovely crisp fivers.'

I explained that it was a 'nothing' price and said I would have given him £60 for the chairs alone.

'Yes but you wouldn't pay £600 for the sideboard, would you, fellah,' chided Tom.

'I thought you said £700,' I replied.

'That's right, you can have it for £700 if you want it,' said Henry. 'That's £100 more than the dealer and his mate are paying me on Saturday.'

'So you haven't got the money yet, then,' I added.

'No,' said Henry. 'He knocked at me door this morning, came in, looked around and couldn't take his eyes off the sideboard. He offered me £400 for it straight out but I said that weren't enough. So he upped it to £500. But I wouldn't take that either, not for a lovely bit of Gothic like that. So he said he'd look round to see if there was anything else he was interested in.'

'Wasn't too keen at first, was he, Henry?' said Rosie.

'Nope, but he liked the set of chairs,' said Henry, 'although he said they weren't worth much – about a fiver each.'

More like fifty each, I thought.

'Anyway, he fiddled around for a bit and had a look at some china and a few brass candlesticks and things. I give him a Bob Luck's and in the end he upped his offer on the Gothic to £600 and said he'd give me £60 for the chairs and other bits. I said I'd want cash and he said that was no problem. Anyway, he took all the chairs and tables and small bits there and then and gave me twelve fivers straight out. He said he'd need help moving the sideboard and he's coming Saturday or Sunday with his mate and £600 in notes. Mind you, if you pay me £700 before then, you can have it instead,' added Henry magnanimously.

I didn't know whether to laugh or cry. There was this smug trio, wallowing in their ignorance, and I just hadn't the heart to tell them they had been taken for a ride by 'knockers' just like the lady with the Bellarmine jar in Chapter 1. Henry would never see these dealers again, or the promised £600 – or, for that matter, his set of chairs, the tables, brassware, postcards and china. But if I had told them that, they would have seen it as a ruse to get the 'Gothic sideboard' for less than £700.

So I finished my cider, asked for another and talked, for the rest of the evening, about anything but antiques. Henry's company was enjoyable, with his tales of early farming days on Romney Marsh and his life at Buckton Farm. And it was no hardship to call again . . . although my next visit was to be one I was to regret bitterly.

It was a Friday evening and all was normal – cider with Henry and tales of his deals in the local livestock market – until the arrival of Tom and Rosie. If I had known Tom better I might have sensed in advance the rather violent edge to his mood that evening. He had wearily sunk into his customary chair on arrival, like a retriever plonking himself in front of the fire after a day in the field. And, just as one leaves sleeping dogs to lie, so also should one leave irritable Toms. Now this, unfortunately, was the night I had agreed to show him my brass clock of *Going for a Song* fame. It rested in a carrier bag at my feet. I saw Tom peeping at the bag occasionally, but he was in no mood to mention the subject to me. So eventually, with an air of indifference (whereas really I was eager to do a deal with it if I could), I said casually: 'By the way, Tom, I brought that clock along with me.'

'Clock, fellah? What clock?'

He knew, of course, but I could see I would have to play the game.

'The one on *Going for a Song*; the brass one.'

'Oh yes, fellah,' replied Tom, feigning a boredom which hid a devious mind bent, right now, on as clever tactics as he could dream up.

45

I took the clock from the carrier bag and handed it to him. I watched Tom and Rosie closely as I did so, and the sparkle in their dark eyes as it emerged from the Sainsbury's bag did not escape me.

'Oh, it's a beauty, Tom' – from Rosie, who had swivelled her plump legs round to gaze at the clock in Tom's lap.

'T'aint so nice as my stable clock' – from Henry, who was shaking more Bob Luck's into his tumbler.

Tom opened the back. 'French movement; eight day,' he said, accurately.

'How much do you want for it then, fellah,' he added with a faint trace of boredom in his voice, trying to kid me he didn't care too much whether he bought it or not.

'Well, you said we might do a deal with some of your items,' I replied. 'But if it's to be cash, as I said before, it's £75, as I paid sixty-five and I've got to make . . .'

My sentence was never completed, because Tom's bull neck reddened and a fearful glint came into his eyes, or at least one of them, the other being clamped shut as he tilted his head and glared at me. In retrospect, he reminded me of nothing so much as Long John Silver about to decapitate one of his crew with a cutlass and 'a yo-ho-ho and a bottle of rum . . .'.

But this was more serious than pirate fiction.

'You told me thirty quid, fellah,' choked Tom, pushing himself to the edge of his seat.

'No, Tom. That's what you *offered*. I told you I paid £65 for it.'

I said it in the tone of a boy up before the Head for smoking.

'You're a liar, fellah,' Tom whispered menacingly this time, the veins in the grooves of his pock-marked face standing out like earthworms. 'SO HELP ME, YOU'RE A LIAR.'

Only this time he was screaming the words at me. And not only was he screaming with rage, he was actually launching his 5ft 3in, but 13 stone, of bone and muscle at me across the room.

'Yes that *is* right, Tom,' piped up Rosie, in rather hushed tones, as though she had witnessed this sort of scene before and knew it was wise to back her husband up.

Henry's hands stopped shaking and his previously flushed face went white.

By now, Tom's contorted features were within two inches of mine. Mine, too, were contorted – with fear. Yes, actual fear that set my whole body shaking, absolutely uncontrollably; there was a dryness in my throat, and a vision of my whole life went reeling through my mind. Clichés or not, these things really do happen.

As Tom gripped my collar with his trench-digging hands, he said: 'If there's one thing I can't stand, fellah, it's a liar. And a liar is what you are, so help me. You'll never lie to me again. You take that back about the £75 or I'll smash this into your face.'

So saying, he pulled back his clenched fist behind him as far as it would go, and Rosie said 'Ooh Tom,' just like Eth used to say 'Ooh Ron' on *Take it From Here*, only this wasn't half so funny.

'But that really is what happened,' I replied. Only the response didn't come out quite like that. I tried to say it three times, failed and could only choke, and the fourth attempt it worked in a pathetic sentence which actually told Tom in so many words, 'I'm scared.'

Tom's face turned from red through purple to blue, and his eyes disappeared under brows that knitted together closer than cable stitch in a Shetland sweater.

'YOU BLOODY LITTLE LIAR,' he screamed at me. 'YOU AGREED TO SELL THAT CLOCK TO ME FOR THIRTY QUID.'

'Make it thirty-five and it's yours,' I quavered.

If that sounds funny now, I was hoping that it would do so at the time I said it, for I had reasoned, in the split second it takes to reason these things when tightly cornered, that perhaps my only chance was to laugh it all off. I also remembered that somewhere in the book of Proverbs it says a mild word turneth away wrath.

So I had said it. And for about five seconds that seemed like five hours I was unsure whether my corpse was going to end up in one of Tom's trenches next week or not.

Then: 'Jesus Christ himself has saved you this evening,' said Tom, trembling himself now, and his voice back in a whisper. And he shoved me backwards into the depths of my armchair, turned, flicked his curly blond hair back off his forehead, straightened his tie and slumped back into his own chair. He glared at me and panted like a man on a life-support machine.

All Rosie could say was: 'Like another cider, Henry?'

47

Henry was shaking again, only this time not with arthritis and war wounds. I think Henry realised, as I did, that we had just escaped carnage.

I remained stiff in my chair, conscious of the thump of my heart within my chest and the still uncontrollable shaking of my whole body. The flare-up had occurred so suddenly and without warning, I felt like the victim of an ambush. And although Wild Man was back in his chair, I did not dare to risk word or movement, lest I re-provoked his unaccountable anger. I could not fathom what he had meant by saying that Jesus had saved me, although I realised quite clearly that He had; there could be no other explanation for the retirement of Tom from the centre of the ring back to his corner.

He was now being ministered to by his 'second' in the form of Rosie, who poured him a cider. Downing it in one gulp, he remained transfixedly staring at me, at the same time taking a tin of Old Holborn and a packet of Rizlas from his pocket; we were like a mongoose and a snake. It was not until he came to lick the cigarette paper that his eyes finally looked away from me. He lit up, inhaled deeply, cupped the butt in his hand, which he let hang between his legs, and thence proceeded to stare at the floor in a hunched position on the edge of his chair. An instinctive understanding of body language told me the crisis was over.

'We'll have to go back and feed the parrot soon,' Rosie said to Tom in a strained voice, looking down into her lap.

'Have another cider first, Tom,' added Henry. 'Goin' over to Buckton Farm in the morning if you'd care to run me down there,' he went on, as though nothing had happened.

'We'll be over at ten,' replied Tom, and his voice shook, requiring deep drags on the Old Holborn to calm what were apparently still highly strung nerves.

Incredibly, it was another forty-five minutes before they left to attend to their starving macaw. Meantime, Henry dispensed more drinks and I eventually plucked up courage to speak. I seem to remember saying inane things like, 'Must be the wettest spell we've had for some time, lately'; or 'I'm probably moving to Scotland next month'. All statements were addressed to Henry, of course, and all were designed to be totally unprovocative, with the latter one a seed I hoped would lodge in Tom's mind to the effect that I wouldn't be seen around much any more. There was no further eye contact with Tom and Rosie.

After the tensest period I can ever remember, including my morning in Sotheby's saleroom, Tom slowly rose from his chair, turned and pulled Rosie from hers as she held her arms out towards him, and they both rather affectionately shuffled out with 'Goodnight, see you in the morning' to Henry and a total ignoring of me. I felt I had witnessed everything on the emotional checklist that evening.

It was perhaps five minutes before Henry said: 'Y'had a lucky escape there y'know. 'E's a devil when e's roused.'

'But what was it all about, Henry?' I asked. 'What I said about the clock was perfectly true.'

''E was just crazy after it. If 'e sees Rosie likes somethin' 'e just has to git it for her. Do anything for that woman, he would.'

'Well why didn't he buy it or do a swap?'

'I'nt got no money, boy, and 'e won't part with anything in 'is place. What goes in there never comes out.'

'So he tried to frighten me into letting him have it for £30, then?'

'Yeah, you're lucky he didn't tear you apart. Did you see where the gas board 'ave got that trench dug on the green near 'is house?' Henry asked.

'I did notice a kind of trench there,' I replied.

'That 'ole's bin there for three months now,' said Henry. 'None of the men'll work on it any more. Not since the day Tom rushed out complainin' of their noise. 'E picked up all of the navvies one after t'other and knocked 'em unconscious into their own pit. None of 'em could stop 'im, he were in that much of a rage; went totally berserk, 'e did. Rosie heard the noise and came out to stop 'im. He was flinging bodies and sods of earth everywhere when she went up and give 'im a good old thump 'erself and Tom ended up in the trench with the others. But 'e just climbed out, docile as one of my young lambs, and trotted back 'ome with 'er. Saw it all out of the bedroom window, I did . . .'

After that, I realised that in future I must only treat with charming old ladies in my quest for antiques. Apart from my evening of terror with Tom, all I ever managed to buy at Henry's during months of trying were two Windsor dining chairs which I sold for £1 each (so you can see they were not much good) and an old lawnmower which I never did get to work. I saw Henry just a couple more times after that evening, weeks later and always when he was alone. The sideboard was still there, of course, and just because I never give up I said to him, 'How much do you want for it, then?'

'I got some dealers comin' for it Saturday, boy. They're givin' me £1,000 for it; if you give me £1,100 cash you can take it away with you tonight . . .'

4
The Lady's Smile

On my many day-long visits to the local country salerooms
where, as you already know, I had the odd bit of luck with Goss
and things, one of the big consolations on summer afternoons
when the bidding was slow and the bargains hard to find was tea
and muffins in one of the many village teashops in the area. The
one I favoured was a delightful Olde English tearoom, with
polished oak tables, warming pans on the walls, plates of hot
scones, and butter shaped in curls. In the window were piles of
homemade sausage rolls and Banbury cakes, and inside the smell
of fresh bread could make you heady with hunger.

And as if that were not enough, one was served by two
delightful-looking girls in white blouses and short skirts, worn
with stockings (I'll swear they weren't tights) and high-heeled
black shoes. Now in case this sounds a bit like an advert for a
storyline to be found in the books favoured by certain shops in
the West End, let me say at once that the two young ladies were
demure and innocent-looking, as wholesome as their toasted
teacakes – or, at least, I thought they were.

Over the weeks I got to know them well, and if I planned my
visits for the slack time just before 3pm, I often found them
sitting on the stairs chatting together, their legs drawn up
provocatively under their chins and girlish laughter ringing
through the shop as they told one another of the secret things
that had happened to them the evening before.

There were often shy looks in my direction as I came in and sat
in my favourite seat by the window, and it occurred to me one
day that I was often the subject of their banter. So I tried smiling
at them, and this worked quite nicely, as Rosemary crossed her
legs on the stairs and June came to serve me tucking in her
blouse. One particular afternoon they both joined me at my table
(I think the proprietor must have been out) and I made them
giggle a bit by acting the fool, which I sometimes don't find hard

to do, and we got chatting very well in between the occasional other customer.

I soon learnt about Rosemary's Baby: it appeared she was an unmarried mother who lived with her mum in a flat in a nearby hamlet; while June, it seemed, had been married a fortnight. Now it occurred to me, from the way things were going, that their own particular domestic situations made not a jot of difference to their very emancipated views on life.

The chatting up was not all one way, for soon they were asking me what I did for a living, and, on being told of my interest in antiques, started taking off various items of jewellery for me to

look at. (Will you forgive me for wishing I travelled in lingerie?) Rosemary had a rather nice gold ring given her by her grandmother, while June's engagement ring must have cost all of £300. They were pleased to learn they were ladies of such substance, and I was treated to extra large portions of apricot jam with my scones.

Over a week or two I became very friendly with both of them and they said my visits cheered them up immensely, while I appreciated the tea and sympathy, not to mention the provocative way two pretty country girls could wear a waitress's uniform.

One afternoon we had been chatting away in the usual manner when June, who had been hovering at the back of the restaurant arranging cutlery and things, came rather shyly over to me and said: 'We've got a proposition to make to you.'

'Oh yes,' I said, reaching for a cigarette despite the fact that I was only halfway through my first round of toast.

'Yes, Rosemary and I need a partner.' She blushed.

So did I, probably, but at the time I was looking at the dollop of butter I had just dropped on my shoe, so possibly she did not notice.

'A partner?' I replied blandly, trying to pretend that my mind was not instantly imagining all sorts of things not usually mentioned in English tearooms. 'What sort of thing had you got in mind?'

'Well,' said June – and I could see Rosemary adjusting her dress in rather embarrassed fashion by the serving hatch – 'well, we need a man.' (And I'll swear she put in a full stop there.) 'To go dancing with.'

'But I can assure you I can't dance,' I said.

'That's great,' said June. 'You see, we'd rather you couldn't, then you can learn the techniques along with us – we're having dancing lessons every Friday night and neither of us has got a partner. We thought you might like to help us out.'

'With the dancing?' I said, with a knowing look in my eye.

'Of course, with the dancing. What else did you think?' said June.

At this, there was a peal of laughter from Rosemary, and June coloured up beautifully.

'Friday's not usually a very good day for me,' I said.

'Stop making excuses,' said Rosemary. 'Come and give us a try this week.'

'Why don't you go with your husband?' I asked June.

'Oh,' she replied vaguely, 'he's a bit of a square about some things. He says dancing makes him feel foolish.'

'Not half so stupid as *you'd* feel dancing with someone like me with four feet,' I replied.

'That's not the point, really,' said Rosemary. 'We thought it would be a bit of fun, as we all seem to get on so well.'

'Well, that's very flattering of you,' I replied. And then, desperately wanting time to work out what was *really* going on, I said I would consider their suggestion while I finished my tea.

'Well, it doesn't matter if you don't want to,' said June, rather sulkily. 'It was only a silly idea we had.'

'No, it wasn't silly,' I said. 'I really am flattered you asked me.'

I recommenced eating my toast, which had now gone cold and soggy, much as I now felt at not having immediately caught the mood of *joie de vivre* of my two young friends. They in turn were rather glumly serving other customers, haughtily disdaining to look in my direction. I was a bit peeved with myself for being such an old square, and after a second cigarette I went up to June at the pay-desk and said, 'Where shall I meet you and what time?'

'Oh good, you're coming, then,' she said, smiling again for the first time in about twenty minutes. 'He's coming,' she called to Rosemary, and I did not miss the wink she tried to hide from me. Rosemary smiled back and said:

'We'll see you outside the village hall Friday evening at 7.30. OK?'

'OK', I replied. 'I'll wear carpet slippers, shall I, they'll be a bit softer if I tread all over you.'

'Promises, promises,' said June, coquettishly. And, as I made my rather selfconscious way out through the door, she added with a wink: 'Don't forget your toothbrush.'

Toothbrush, I thought. Toothbrush? And as I did a double-take I caught a reflection in the restaurant window of a man rather pleased with himself but at the same time not a trifle apprehensive. The reflection was my own!

So now I had to put the action where my mouth was. This will

54

teach you to chat up girls half your age, my boy, I told myself.

I must admit the closer Friday evening got, the more apprehensive I became. I told myself, on the one hand, that it was just a bit of innocent fun; and then, on the other hand, I recalled the look in June's eye when she said the bit about the toothbrush. Supposing her husband was bigger than me!

Anyway, Friday evening eventually arrived — which is a rather obvious statement to make, although I had half persuaded myself that if I ignored it, it might not happen. Now it's true that I didn't have to go, but I could never have looked myself in the eye again if I had backed down, so at 7pm I got in the car and drove to the village. Not having had dancing lessons for about twenty years, I had no idea what would be considered suitable attire. So I was wearing a suit of sober cut, shirt and tie, I had shined my shoes and slicked my hair, as they say in the song, and was altogether rather got up like the proverbial dog's dinner.

At 7.25 I arrived at my destination and made for the vicinity of the village hall. As it had occurred to me these high-spirited young ladies could actually have been taking me for a gigantic ride, and I did not wish to appear foolish lest they were not there, I decided to approach the meeting place circumspectly, so that if there was no one about at the appointed hour I could make my getaway without losing too much face, except perhaps with myself. It was a wise decision.

I stopped the car behind a Post Office van which was conveniently parked twenty-five yards from the village hall. Winding down the driver's window of my car, I peered cautiously but curiously out. No one about. 'Thought so,' I muttered to myself. 'You've let your vanity take you for a ride.'

I sat there for a few minutes, feeling foolish, when I heard the sound of distant footsteps. Looking up into my rear-view mirror, I saw rounding a corner two young ladies bearing a slight resemblance to June and Rosemary. That they actually *were* June and Rosemary was not immediately obvious. For gone were the smart but rather prissy waitresses' uniforms, and gone too were the slightly provocative but rather formal facades of the girls I knew of the tearooms. And in their place were prancing along the tree-clad high street of a middle class village two absolute ravers. June was teetering on a pair of four-inch heels which made walking hazardous but highly interesting; she wore a split skirt in black and a green blouse with the top five buttons undone. Rosemary, on the other hand, had on the tightest pair of jeans I had ever seen, which in turn were tucked into thigh-length brown boots; the whole lot was topped by a red sweater which clung intimately to every curve of her very substantial upper half. Easing my by now rather hot little hands down the creases of my *Come Dancing* suit, I quickly realised that the last thing June and Rosemary were going to do in *their* outfits was ballroom dancing. Why, Victor Sylvester would have turned — albeit slow, slow, quick, quick, slow — in his grave.

And as I saw them in the mirror bouncing nearer and nearer to me, I noticed that June was carrying a transistor radio and a bottle wrapped in off licence tissue paper, while Rosemary had a duffle bag and what looked suspiciously like a ground-sheet!

Now, it occurred to me that the big joke was going to be that I would go up to them outside the village hall and they would look right through me as though they had never seen me before, and I would turn round and see two village bucks step out of an MGB or something equally flash. The girls would wave, then wobble their way into the dicky seat and I would be covered in a cloud of dust as the young lovers screeched off with burning tyres into the sunset. But no, it was to transpire that I had been watching too many cheap movies. For as the girls approached the back of my car, I ducked down between the front seats until they had gone past, and I watched them walk into the village hail car park. Rosemary checked her watch, while I saw June click on the transistor radio, whereupon they both started jiving on the spot with gyrating hips and bobbing heads as Radio 1 blared out into the silence of a spring evening in a Kentish village.

No sports cars arrived and it soon became apparent they really were waiting for *me*.

All sorts of thoughts flashed through my mind. Yes, all the ones you can imagine, plus one or two others that my guardian angel threw in for good measure — like visions of nasty scenes at the divorce courts or, at the very least, being left holding Rosemary's baby. So in a moment which took — I think — real courage, I turned my ignition key, selected first gear and shot off down the high street as fast as my Mark II Cortina would take me. Which was not as fast as an MGB would have made it, so it enabled June and Rosemary to catch sight of me as I flashed past the village hall. At first they waved as I approached, then, seeing me continue at great pace down the high street, they wheeled round on their sexy heels, with June raising her left fist and shaking it at my receding rear end, while Rosemary, I saw in the mirror, flung her duffle bag and ground-sheet down in disgust. And then they both stood glaring with legs apart and hands on their hips, as I selected third gear at 60 mph and took the bend at the far end of the high street.

So I learnt that it was more than saleroom bargains that you could pick up in this little village. But I paid quite a price for the information, for understandably I could never again dare go for tea and homemade scones in a certain olde English country tearoom.

* * * * * * * *

I am glad to say this incident did not put me off continuing my career as an unashamed Romantic. Not so long afterwards, in a local antiques and secondhand shop, I met and fell in love with a beautiful lady. I passed her on the stairs, and she half smiled at me. I knew I could not leave her there in her unhappy situation, so I smiled back, and took her home. And as I write these words she looks across the room at me, for we are still together, and her smile is now one of completeness.

Sad to say, it was not always so, for her previous keeper had not cherished her in the manner such a graceful lady deserved, and her mouth and neck had flaked away. For my beautiful friend is an oil on canvas, a portrait of the Victorian era, probably of the Italian school.

Even as she hung damaged on the dingy back staircase of the shop, I could see that she had been painted by a good professional artist, probably commissioned by her husband or lover. The painting was in a superb gilt frame which, alone, was worth four or five times what was asked for the painting, so I knew I could not go wrong, even if it proved impossible to get the portrait restored.

I had it in the back of my mind to ask my good friend Leslie Atkinson, husband of the doll lady from Canterbury, to see if he could restore her to her former glories. Leslie was a painter himself and had been a professional book illustrator before retiring to run an antiques shop with his wife. But it seemed to me it would be quite a task.

In fact the painting languished in my garage for a long time before I approached Leslie about restoration work – so long, in fact, that the Atkinsons had retired from business to a lovely old country house near Petworth by the time I got round to making my request.

It was a beautiful spring day as I drove through Sussex lanes yellow with primroses on my way to their new home. When I showed Leslie the painting he made a close examination of the damage, which he said had been caused by damp making the paint flake off, before pronouncing the task difficult but not totally out of the question.

'Leave her with me for the summer,' he said, 'and I'll see what I can do.' I agreed.

Many months went by and I had almost forgotten about her, when I had a card from Leslie one October day saying: 'The Mona Lisa smiles again; come and collect, any time.'

So this time I set off down Sussex lanes burnished with autumn gold from a million leaves glinting in an Indian summer's warm light. And there, hanging in the Atkinsons' huge lounge, was my lovely friend, smiling prettily down at me as though the problems of life had never touched her.

It seemed to me nothing short of a miraculous work of restoration, so I asked Leslie to tell me how the job had been accomplished.

The first task he told me, had been to secure the canvas to its wooden frame, or stretcher, since it had split along two of its edges. This operation was easily performed with a little plastic glue and extra tacks around the edges. Now that the canvas was taut, the whole surface could be wiped over with white spirit to remove superficial dirt.

Next, the more difficult operation of filling the large central area damaged by damp was carried out. An impasto (thick layers of oil paint) mixed with gilder's putty was first used, but as this would not dry satisfactorily, Leslie resorted to Polyfilla.

'This,' he explained, 'is a convenient modern equivalent of gesso, a mixture of gypsum (plaster of Paris) with size which the old masters used as a ground when painting in egg tempera, over which they later applied glazes in oil paint, circa 1430, before finally changing to oil paints exclusively from the sixteenth century onwards. This new white area of filling was then covered with a flesh-coloured priming coat mixed with varnish to seal its surface.'

Leslie's next task was to clean the dirty varnish from the lady's face and to uncover the flesh tones so that they could be matched accurately. 'I used Winsor and Newton's picture cleaner applied with cotton-wool swabs. I thought more extensive cleaning would remove the picture's antique flavour,' he said.

Next, Leslie drew the outline of the mouth, chin and shadow under the chin with a fine brush. 'The lady's lace collar and brooch had to be redesigned, as they had almost totally disappeared,' he said. 'Then came the trickiest bit – matching the colours. I'd do the painting and leave it in the sun only for it to dry too light in colour. It was only by extensive trial and error that I finally got it right.'

'The mouth (which along with the eyes is the most difficult part of a face to draw) gave me constant problems and in the end I was forced to use an acquaintance as a model. She had just the right mouth and chin and at last I was able to get it right.

'To speed up the drying process I mixed the oil pigments with turpentine instead of linseed oil. To make the newly-painted area blend with the original glossy appearance I used retouching varnish over the whole picture area rather than a finishing varnish. The whole of the dress I repainted in a purple plum colour, which I think was an improvement on the original black. I then used the craquelure process on the dress to imitate the original cracks; I didn't do this on the face as, having spent so many hours getting it right, I did not want to risk ruining it,' added Leslie. Finally, retouching varnish was applied over the whole canvas.

The painting is unsigned and undated, but during the restoration some interesting facts emerged. The flesh textures were painted with a stipple technique rather like that of the Post Impressionist Seurat, who was working in the late nineteenth century. But Leslie had never seen the technique used in an English painting of the period of mine (c 1860). Stippling was originally an engraver's technique. It was invented by an Italian, Bartolozzi (1728-1815), who moved to England in 1764 and was appointed engraver to George III; he was an original member of the Royal Academy. This knowledge led Leslie to conclude that the painter of the lady's portrait was an Italian, probably someone who had been influenced by Bartolozzi's engraving technique.

Certainly, the lady does have an Italian look about her. But whoever painted her, and whoever loved her enough to want such a painting done, it is Leslie Atkinson who has made her smile again, and it is I who love her now. I am glad we met and smiled at one another in that country secondhand shop.

5
My Jolly Good Friend the Dustman Said . . .

I once cleared a house near Lymington, Hampshire, of its contents, and this necessitated several trips to the nearby council tip to dispose of a number of items of no use to man nor beast – no beast, that is, except the variety that appeared to dwell on this particular tip. Dressed in the checked shirts of colourful hue which seem to have become the uniform of Country and Western groups, adorned with gold earrings, Elvis Presley haircuts and brothel creepers to match, the diddicoy pack spent the days – and possibly nights as well – awaiting the next carload of cast-offs to pick over. Whether six years old or sixty, every member of the gang looked much the same, lounging beside the numerous bonfires that burnt around the site. They reminded me of funeral pyres – which is what, in a way, they were. No bodies were being burnt (although, looking at the gang, I wouldn't swear to that) but the items that smouldered with choking smoke were mainly from the homes of those recently deceased.

On my first visit to the dump, the scavengers stood rather respectfully back as I chucked old mattresses and things on to the bonfires. But with each subsequent trip they became bolder, until after the third visit they were actually climbing into the back of my van before I had time even to stop the engine. They swarmed over the tailgate like rats up a plank, cursing and swearing over anything they could not sell again for a bob or two, and then rather naively asked me if some plated ashtrays in a paper bag were silver. I told them they were, whereupon they went straight into the gang leader's jacket pocket. On the next trip, when they found absolutely nothing of any value, they became so abusive that I feared I myself would finish up on a bonfire. I wondered whether my gold fillings would save me, but decided the best thing to do was find another dump.

Now, although I have expressed distaste at these proceedings, I do so only at the manner of this gang's doings rather than the

61

motives behind them. That a group of diddicoys could make a handsome living from other people's rubbish surprised me not one bit. On occasions I have made a few bob that way myself. In this chapter are one or two such tales, all perfectly true, that may really surprise you.

I first became aware of what little goldmines rubbish dumps can be following my observation of an elderly woman who took a baby in a pram for a walk round her local rubbish dump every

evening at 6pm, when the workmen had gone home. This struck me as odd for two rather obvious reasons: first, she seemed, from her demeanour, to be rather past her prime breeding condition; and second, a council tip was a little on the eccentric side as a place for perambulations with a babe in swaddling clothes. However, on closer examination one evening I noticed that they were not actually swaddling clothes but old wraps containing little bundles of brass and china and more than useful household gadgets that she had found. Then, one Tuesday when I arrived early at Moses' sale, I saw the same woman push her old pram into the saleroom to disgorge a nice selection of pickings from the tip which went on to fetch some rather rewarding prices. Indeed, I bought one or two of them myself.

I hope I may be believed when I say that it was not just the lack of a pram that prevented me joining in these fun and games myself. I mean, we all have standards to keep up, haven't we? But as luck would have it, within a couple of weeks I was to find a much better source of supply than the tip itself.

Two Tuesdays later, when Mr Moses had knocked down a number of brass and copper items to me (much to the annoyance of half a dozen other saleroom regulars whose continued bidding had been ignored by the redoubtable auctioneer), I was approached after the sale by a short man in a tatty tweed suit who spoke out of one corner of his mouth, while in the other he clamped a damp and tarry fag-end. He was, I guessed, in his mid-fifties.

'See you bought most of my bits today,' he muttered conversationally.

'Yes, old Moses seems to have taken a liking to me this week. I thought they were pretty reasonable.'

'Oh, yes?' queried Fag-end. 'Be interested in a few more bits, cheap?'

'Always on the look-out for anything at the right price.'

'Well, come over my place one evening. Might have a few things to interest you.'

'OK,' I said. 'Tonight all right?'

'Half past seven. Not before, I shall be having me dinner,' said Fag-end, giving me his address on a small council estate not far away.

Pondering the advantages of always chatting to people, even the most unlikely looking characters, I spent the afternoon cleaning my bits of brass and copper ware and wondering what delights might await me in a council house shed that evening.

Prompt at 7.30 I knocked on the rather shabby green door of the house in question. A child's tricycle, three carboys, a World War II helmet, three wellington boots and half a rotting cream sponge in a box lay in the porch. Had I known it, they gave quite a clue to the occupation of the tenant. But I had no time to think of this before the door was opened by a thin young woman in her twenties in a mini-skirt which revealed legs that would have failed to stop a pig in a passage, and a tight white blouse out of which peeped disproportionately large breasts.

'Is your dad in?' I inquired.

'Me dad's dead. Who d'ya' want?' she asked, pulling the top of her blouse together with her left hand.

'Oh, sorry,' I said, trying to ignore the little dribbles of milk that were now staining the blouse. 'I had an appointment to see a chap I met in the market this morning; said he'd got some bits and pieces for sale — you know, brass and things.'

'That's me husband,' she said. 'He's in the kitchen having his tea. Come through.'

She led the way into the back parlour, where Fag-end was perched on the edge of a sofa through one end of which poked a spring. He was poised between stuffing half a sausage into his mouth and guffawing at a rather feeble joke in a TV commercial. His wife stuck a cushion over the menacing spring, sat down and picked up an infant from an old black pram beside the telly and proceeded to feed it from swollen, milk-oozing breasts now totally removed from her blouse.

Looking politely towards the flickering TV screen, I said: 'Sorry, I seem to be a bit early.'

There was no reply from the woman or from Fag-end, who watched the end of the beer commercial with the intensity of a dog waiting for a morsel from its master. Which was exactly the real situation, for the man threw the last quarter-inch of his sausage to a mongrel that leaped savagely from a cardboard box across the room, devouring the titbit with one chomp of its vicious little mouth.

'I'll have me cuppa now, woman,' said Fag-end, his eyes still glued to the flickering screen.

There was a plop as her reddened nipple fell from the by-now comatose infant's mouth. With some dexterity, she poured from a teapot perched on an oak trolley with a wheel missing.

'See if the man'd like one,' ordered Fag-end.

The woman looked at me with a quizzical expression on a rather sullen face that seemed to have been lived in far beyond her actual age.

'Yes, please. Plenty of milk and no sugar if you don't mind,' I said.

'Anything you like,' she said, seductively, replacing one of her breasts in her blouse.

It struck me that it was probably a phrase like that, uttered one abandoned spring evening behind the council estate garages, that may have precipitated her current rather depressing domestic situation with Fag-end, a chap thirty years her senior but who, despite his present benign posture, was obviously still an active man with an eye for the crumpet.

'Like some cake with it?' asked Fag-end, who was now dunking the baby's Farley's rusks into his own cuppa and sucking them noisily between the gaps in his front teeth.

'Wouldn't mind,' I replied cheerfully, quite prepared to share this rather unpretentious after-dinner situation.

'It's in the porch, woman. Go and get it, will you. Might have a bit myself.'

You may perhaps imagine how my heart, not to say my stomach, sank to my boots as I remembered the mouldering cream sponge I had spotted on my way in. I simply watched with disbelief as the woman ambled off in the direction of the front door. Presently I heard the clink of plates from the kitchen, then she re-emerged bearing four slices of cream sponge on a dinner plate. The dusting of icing sugar on the top had a kind of eczema which I guessed had been caused by spots of rain, and where the cream and raspberry filling had oozed out there were little specks of dust stuck there like flies on a newly distempered wall.

'Er, sorry, sorry,' I said, unable to take my eyes from the confection. 'Looks ever so nice but didn't realise it was a cream cake,' I went on desperately. 'Can't eat cream, I'm afraid. Got an allergy to dairy produce. Brings me out in a rash. It does look nice, though, but really I must resist.'

'Cor, love us,' said Fag-end, reaching for the largest slice, which he squeezed in a grubby fist before placing the whole lot into his mouth. 'That's Lyons' best cream sponge, that is. Came from a good home and all – one of the big houses down Cassiobury Lane.'

'Er, you mean someone was kind enough to give it to you?' I queried, rather relieved to see another slice follow the first down Fag-end's throat.

'In a manner of speaking, yes,' he said. 'Often get a nice bit of something or other from "Greenbanks", don't we, love?' he went on, patting his wife's thigh as she, too, bit into a slice of this revolting sponge.

'Do you know the "Greenbanks" people, then?' I asked, conversationally.

'In a manner of speaking, yes,' replied Fag-end. 'Usually call in once a week.'

'Oh, must be nice,' I said, trying not to retch.

'All in the line of duty,' said Fag-end vaguely. 'Got to get your perks where you can.'

'Perks?' I said.

'Yes, gotta get your bits and pieces where you can, these days. People are keeping hold of things longer. Everything costs so much now.'

Completely puzzled, I said: 'Sounds a fascinating job. What do you do?'

'I'm on the council. A foreman on the council.'

''E means 'e's a dustman,' said the woman bitterly from the other end of the sofa, joining in the conversation.

'I ain't a dustman, woman. I'm a foreman.'

'Same thing. Just means you don't pick up the bins any more. I've seen you – you just point where they have to tip the rubbish in the rear of the waggon and help the driver back up alleys.'

'Yes, but that's a responsible job; they don't have any old bloke as a foreman, you know. And anyhow, I get the pick of all the best bits the punters have thrown out. I don't see you grumbling when I bring home a decent saucepan or two for the kitchen, woman.'

Then, turning to me: 'Look at the stuff I've got in this place, mate. Shouldn't think I've paid a penny piece for any of it,' he said proudly.

'Very nice,' I said, trying to disguise the slight pain I was experiencing at a sofa spring that was niggling at a delicate part of my anatomy.

'Cooker, fridge, kitchen table and four chairs, sofa, tea trolley, beds, a wardrobe — I've had them all off the round. Most of it Cassiobury Lane stuff. Good quality, all of it. Some women don't know when they're well off.'

'Well off!' said the woman, sulkily. 'I need an anaesthetic to pull me drawers up after sitting on this sofa for half an hour.'

'Bah, women,' said Fag-end, throwing the fourth slice of sponge to the mongrel.

The dog caught the cake expertly in its jaws and promptly dropped it again on the carpet. It then gazed at it with a desultory look on its face.

'Blimey, don't *you* get fussy, dog,' said the foreman dustman. 'Come on, mate, let's have a look in the shed. Might be a few bits we can do a deal on.'

So saying, he led me down the garden path.

Once inside, I wondered if he hadn't actually led me *up* the garden path, for at first sight I could see nothing of the remotest interest to an antique dealer. There was a pile of rotting *Woman's Own* magazines in a corner, a broken fish tank, several dozen flower pots, two chairs with broken cane seats, a pressure cooker, an electric stove with no elements, three sandals, an estate agent's board, two rolls of chicken wire and a box containing an old truss.

'Any of this any good to you?' inquired Fag-end hopefully.

'Er, well,' I hesitated, 'there's nothing very old here except the truss and I should think that would have to go to London.'

'Oh,' said Fag-end. 'What about the magazines, then? Quite a market for old magazines these days, I believe.'

'Yes, there can be,' I said. 'Trouble is I've not had much luck with *Woman's Own* just lately; the market seems to have gone quiet all of a sudden.'

Fag-end looked thoughtful.

'Well, that's about all I've got at the moment, mate. There's a

67

few bits and pieces in the front room, but nothing to interest you, I shouldn't think.'

'Never know your luck,' I replied. 'Let's have a look.'

So we marched back up the path past some rotting brussels sprouts plants and a small pond full of plastic toys.

'Shell cases, mate. Got stacks of shell cases. Clean up nice for umbrella stands.'

Fag-end was showing me some empty brass cases from World War II which, it was true, were quite in vogue as doorstops and walking-stick receptacles.

'Cassiobury Lane?' I asked.

'No, mate, dug them up down the Marsh.'

'How much each, then?'

'Fiver.'

'Oh, no, couldn't possibly. Only get £3.50 for them myself.'

'Well, you're selling them too cheap, mate. One dealer I have comes here regular and gives me £6.'

'Should save them for him, then, if I were you.'

'Four quid, then?'

'No. Two's the best I can go.'

'OK. Two quid each. You're a hard man.'

'Any other brass or copper?' I asked.

'Got an old kettle, not much use.'

So saying, Fag-end produced a beautiful little Georgian kettle from the sideboard which he described as no good to man nor beast. A small hole in the bottom meant it wouldn't hold water any more.

I expressed regret, although the last thing I was thinking of using it for was brewing up my Earl Grey. I offered £2.

'Blimey, you could have had it for 50p.'

'OK, 50p then, I've no pride!' I said.

Diving into the sideboard again, Fag-end produced what he called a collapsible tray. 'Can't find out what it's for. Something medical, I should think.'

The collapsible tray turned out to be a delightful folding cake-stand of the Victorian era in perfect condition.

''Tis a bit of a puzzle,' I said. 'Should be worth something as scrap, though. Three quid all right?'

'Take it.'

Next the sideboard produced an album of postcards.

'Took the stamps off some of these cards,' said Fag-end. 'Not much use, though – all pennies and three-halfpennies. Looked 'em up in me catalogue; all worth 10p each. You can have the rest for a quid.' Then:

'Here you are: hop tokens. Don't see them about much now, do you? Three quid the lot?'

Then into the kitchen to view a brass coal-hod and an old coal-box. The early Victorian coal-hod of helmet shape was gathering drips under the sink. Removing a Wonderloaf from an Edwardian rosewood coal cabinet inlaid with boxwood, Fag-end suggested: 'Six quid the two?'

I was by now utterly amazed at all the apparently unconsidered trifles that were secreted about the dustman's council house rooms.

'That's it, then,' said Fag-end. 'Won't have no more till next week. No, hold on, I was forgetting: it's Easter next week, they won't be chucking much out save chocolate boxes and turkey carcasses. Always a bit quiet, Easter is. Come round in a fortnight.'

'You mean all this stuff came off your round?' I asked.

'Where else, mate? You don't think I nicked this old rubbish, do you?'

'Certainly not,' I reassured him. 'I'm just amazed at what people throw away.'

'Well, it's not worth anything much is it?' asked Fag-end, a perplexed look on his face. 'Me best stuff's down the shed, but you didn't want it.'

'It was so kind of you to offer,' I said desperately, trying not to give the game away. 'I just find these old things a bit more quaint and interesting, that's all.'

'Well, it takes all sorts,' said Fag-end with a shrug.

As Fag-end led me down the hall to the front door, I'll swear I heard the sounds of plosive evacuation from an upstairs room. Passing through the porch I noticed the Lyons cake carton had indeed disappeared from among the wellington boots, carboys and World War II helmet. Privately congratulating myself on conquering my normal weakness for cream cakes, I said, above the noises from upstairs: 'Two weeks' time, then. I'll call round again to see what you've got. Thanks for the bits and pieces and, er, the cup of tea.'

'Pleasure, mate,' replied Fag-end. 'You must come and have a bite to eat next time.'

* * * * * * * *

I can report, very thankfully indeed, that although I called on my jolly good friend the dustman many times again, never once did I have a bite to eat. I had a few cups of tea, but only after establishing that they were prepared with real tea-leaves and not tea-bags, on the basis that, if the latter, they could have been part of some mind-boggling recycling scheme devised by Fag-end and his corporation crew.

I made some very good buys there, too, and was constantly amazed that the man filled his home with some appalling kitsch of which he seemed so proud, at the same time selling for a song some very desirable items indeed about which he knew nothing and cared less.

The strange thing was that after a couple of visits I found out that there really was another dealer who called regularly and that Fag-end hadn't invented a mythical rival to gee me up into paying better money. And it transpired that the other dealer was my friend Robert.

This became apparent when Robert was telling me one day of the amazing little buy he had had of silver coins which he had located in a council house bedroom. The chap had had some sovereigns, as well, which apparently he wasn't selling at the moment, but Robert was persevering with his supplier who, he said, was a dustman with not a lot up top – except in his bedroom.

One little hint led to another and before long I was saying to Robert, 'Doesn't live in Hoylake Avenue, by any chance, does he?'

'Yes, don't say *you* know him?' said Robert, his face sinking.

'As a matter of fact I've been calling there regularly myself just lately,' I said smugly. 'Met up with him at Moses' in the market.'

Robert looked at me as though secretly I'd been rummaging through his private address book. This wasn't the first, nor was it the last, occasion our paths were to cross in the rather devious

70

ways that dealers' often do. But apart from anything else, I didn't know where Robert *kept* his private address book!

Well, I think he believed me in the end. At least we came to a friendly agreement about who bought what from Fag-end. I was to purchase anything going on the nights I called, and Robert likewise on the occasions he dropped in, with the proviso that if the sovereigns were ever sold, Robert had first chance to buy. From then on, however, my friend seemed to get advance knowledge of any good pickings Fag-end had had, because for many weeks afterwards, whenever I called at the council house, I seemed to be greeted with the same old cry: 'Sorry, mate, nothing much for you this week. Had a dealer in yesterday, cleared me out . . . .' Which is exactly how Robert came to make one of his biggest killings – a fine English bracket clock of the Regency period which he later confessed he had acquired for a song (£20, I think it was) on one of his visits to Fag-end.

A Regency bracket clock is, of course, quite a late example of this type of timepiece. They were thought to have developed from about 1670 onwards, being a natural successor to brass lantern clocks, sometimes called Cromwellian clocks, which were themselves the earliest type of clock case made in England. They were also known as 'birdcage' clocks, maybe because of their domed top. With the introduction of the pendulum into English clock movements about 1660, giving greater accuracy than its predecessor, the balance wheel, lantern clocks had to be fixed on walls or placed on brackets so that the pendulum and weights could swing below. So when their successors, the wooden-cased bracket clocks, came into vogue in the late seventeenth century it was natural that they, too, should stand on brackets – hence the term 'bracket clocks'. Their cases developed slowly over the next hundred years or so, commencing with square faces and hoods, later adopting inverted bell tops, arch tops, balloon cases, gadroon tops, and so on. But no one style seemed to supersede another and designs of the eighteenth century were still common during the nineteenth. Of course, with the development of clock movements there soon came to be no need for weights and pendulums to swing underneath but nevertheless these clocks still retained their position on brackets. And with the introduction of the lever escapement to replace pendulums, a

71

fashion began for miniature mantel clocks in restricted cases too narrow to permit the swing of a pendulum.

As far as Robert's clock was concerned, an examination of the movement indicated that it was probably of the Regency period, and none the worse for that. Apparently the foreman-dustman had offered it to him one evening. He had said he had an old clock which wasn't much use, as it didn't go. His gang had found it lying on the top of a bin on their rounds that week outside a fairly well-to-do house whose owners obviously had more money than sense. As Robert in those days always had more sense than money, he had happily paid out the £20 demanded by Fag-end (a price, incidentally, that proved the old boy had a sixth sense that it might be worth a bob or two, as normally his asking price for almost anything was no more than a fiver).

Robert had the movement restored by a professional clock repairer and sold it for a very handsome profit to a country dealer who was quite delighted to pay a few hundred pounds for a timepiece that he in his turn was going to pass on for a further substantial mark-up. Fag-end had been delighted with the price he had asked for and received, so everyone was happy. Well, as he said himself, 'It takes all sorts.' And there's no doubt at all that Robert, like me, is a lucky 'sort'.

To conclude this chapter on the amazing things that find their way on to rubbish tips, let me relate what Robert found on the top of a dustbin before it had even been tipped into the back of the corporation dustcart. Driving down the main street of a sleepy little Kentish village one afternoon, Robert – who seems to have more eyes than an old potato – spotted some gilt frames and a carrier-bag or two lying alongside a dustbin outside the front gate of an old cottage. Not one to pass by such things without investigation, he poked around amid the rubbish and found three oil paintings – two still-lifes and an attractive seascape. Always one to observe a modicum of manners, Robert knocked at the door of the cottage and inquired of the rather prim woman who came to the door whether, as they were destined for the tip anyway, he could have the three dirty old pictures they were throwing out.

'Oh, yes,' Miss Prim had replied. 'We really don't want any of this awful old stuff now Mother's died. We've had a jolly good clear-out already. Modernising, you know. Really, you wouldn't believe some of the dreadful old things Mother kept. Must have been First World War, most of it.'

'Oh,' Robert had said, sensing a killing. 'Anything else you don't want?'

'Well, I'm afraid you're too late, young man, the secondhand furniture dealer in the village had the rest yesterday,' said Miss Prim.

But Robert, being Robert, was not too late at all. He grabbed the three unwanted paintings and drove hell-for-leather down to the secondhand shop. Here he concluded a nice little deal with the owner, with whom he occasionally did business anyway, which saw a number of items enter his stockbook that proved beyond any doubt that Miss Prim's old mother had had far better taste than her modern young daughter.

I saw the three paintings. There were two excellent still lifes of fruit of the mid-nineteenth century English school, professionally painted and fitting very well into the scheme of things in the front room of Robert's cottage. I much admired the seascape, too, before it was admired even more at the front desk at a top London auctioneers. They identified it as the work of Ludolph Backhuysen, an eminent master born at Emden in 1631, whose favourite subject was sea pieces. It was the custom of the artist to persuade hardy mariners to take him out to sea during storms where, amid the tossing waves, he absorbed the atmosphere for his chiaroscuro technique.

I have often wondered what he would have thought had he known that 300 years later his work would be tossed into a village dustbin.

Ah, well, it takes all sorts.

6
Mad Dogs and Englishmen

If it seems a trifle eccentric of Robert and me to go around buying things that people have chucked into their dustbins – and any perfectly normal person would think so – the fact is that an antiques dealer in the country finds himself in all manner of unlikely places and predicaments.

You have already heard how I filled my cottage with all sorts of bric-à-brac in the hope that seaside-bound holidaymakers would pop in for a bargain or two. That was quite normal. There were a few minor problems, of course. If you have a grandfather clock in the second bedroom, a set of Regency chairs in the garage and some First Period Worcester in the lavatory, you have to be some kind of Houdini to keep an eye on all your bits as a party of potential buyers spreads out round your rooms. And, of course, the beds had to be made pretty sharply of a morning.

There was also Sam, our labrador, who had to be watched even more keenly than the customers. The normal ritual was to slip the loop of his lead under a bed-post – preferably a pretty strong bed-post – when a car was heard coming up the drive. Otherwise he would race through the cottage at the first sound of approaching footsteps, scattering everything in his path like a drunken man in an egg-packing station. Nothing could stop him and he would hurl himself at the back door and shake with anger at the petrified faces that peeped back at him round the lintel. Provided they didn't run, they were OK! Frankly, I think most of them were too scared to move. Mind you, as a precaution we fed him well.

On the occasions when he was safely attached to the end of the bed, Sam served as a reliable indicator of who would buy and who would not. If he barked and growled at whoever was in the lounge admiring my coal-hod or whatever, I knew that person would escape without having to part with money – and, hopefully, the seat of his pants! If, however, the yapping

74

subsided into a friendly sniff under the gap in the door, that was a sure sign that I was about to make a sale. Sam rarely let me down, and no sooner had I taken the money and seen my customer down to the gate than I would go into the bedroom to slip Sam's lead and find him fast and contentedly asleep at the bottom of the bed, his whiskers twitching and his legs jerking as he dreamt of his walk in the woods last night when he chased squirrels up old oak trees and scented his girl-friend by the farm gate.

My wife, Joy, was a valuable aid in keeping an eye on people, at the same time interesting them in the bits and pieces in which she had taken a personal interest. Her particular forte was kitchen equipment, but woe betide anyone who tried to buy the

jugs, plates and old coffee grinders and things which she had kept for herself. At salerooms, too, she would often spot an interesting old thing that I had overlooked. So as not to draw too much attention to what she had spotted, we had a kind of code: she would roll her long elegant fingers on a side-table or something to draw my attention, and then quietly point to her discovery, raising her eyebrows with a quizzical expression as much as to say, 'What do you think of this?' One of her best finds was an elegant Victorian marble-topped washstand on turned legs, in mahogany, which she spotted hidden away down 'The Tatty'. Being partly obscured, I had been able to buy it for 20p, a ridiculous price for an item worth at least £15 then and about £45 nowadays. Joy lived up to her name.

She is also a woman who loves polishing: copper, brass, silver or just the kitchen floor — you name it, she'll polish it. That, you will appreciate, is a great asset in an antique dealer's wife. A lady of good taste, she is expert at summing up the merits of old jewellery. I once bought an old 'brass' chain for a fiver which Joy soon told me was 18ct gold, having located a minute hallmark on one of the links. I sold it for £150 in 1977 and suppose that with the mad escalation in the price of gold three years later, it would have fetched £500 to £600. Anyway, I should grumble.

I suppose one of the worst things that happened at the cottage was the day I saw a huddle of people at the bottom of the drive, their hands raised to their mouths and wide-eyed with horror as they gazed at my chicken run. I dashed out to find blood spraying everywhere like something out of the last five minutes of *Kojak*. My two cockerels had somehow got at each other through two layers of 2 inch mesh wire fencing and were fighting to the death in a pen full of cowering hens and a garden full of cowering customers. The fiery little bantam cock which my eldest son Graham had bought for 50p from the farmer down the road had the other bird, twice his size, by the comb and was dashing his head against the ground. The engorged comb was spurting blood over everything, including the overcoats of my customers. The women were white-faced and whimpering 'Stop them, stop them,' and the men were saying things like, 'This is outrageous; supposed to be a civilised country.'

I grabbed a nearby bean pole and beat the bantam cock off, at the same time explaining that this, I could assure them, was not part of the normal rural entertainment in this neck of the woods and that, if they would care to make their way to the kitchen, I would get the blood off in just a moment if they would only give me a minute or two to stop the carnage. I also thought that if they were in the kitchen they would not notice my own apprehension at having to deal with this 1½lb bundle of fury. In the end, the only way I could get the birds apart was by tipping cold water over them out of the watering can. This seemed to dampen their ardour and also served to staunch the flow of blood from wounds inflicted by two sets of vicious spurs.

I then helped my visitors clean up, whereupon they beat a hasty retreat back to their car, muttering all the way to the gate about country people being back in the Middle Ages. I expected a call from the village bobby for a week afterwards, for I was sure my visitors imagined the cockfight had been a little diversion I had been enjoying that particular drowsy summer afternoon when trade was slack and this bumpkin antique dabbler had sought to relieve the boredom. But nothing happened except that a few days later the bigger of the two cockerels found its way into the pot, where the sweetness of its flesh atoned somewhat for the bitterness I felt at its lame performance in the cockpit.

But apart from things like that and the occasional herd of bullocks chewing my grass in the small hours, ours was a fairly normal establishment, at least by comparison with those of other country antiques dealers. I shall never know how a fellow dealer made a living up in the hills of the Weald. I had heard that he, too, sold from his home in a little cottage – fine English porcelain of the eighteenth century, so rumour had it. One spring morning I set off in search of his dwelling and drove up into the Downs through lanes billowing with may blossom that scattered like confetti in the gentle breeze that fluttered over Kentish meadows strutting with peewits. Angry blackbirds scolded me from tangled cottage gardens down rustic tracks as I knocked at countless doors inquiring for the dealer in early English porcelain. Kindly faced cottagers were at pains to explain to me that if it was Lowestoft and Worcester I was after then probably I was in the wrong county. I tried tactfully explaining that I didn't actually want to go to Lowestoft, Chelsea or Derby, merely buy some of the products of their old factories. But bless their hearts, as warm as the lazy log fires in their grates, I just could not make them understand. So by mid-afternoon I drove back from the Downs through elder-scented lanes without having had so much as a sniff at old English china. But somewhere up in those hills is a dealer with rooms stuffed full of blue and white and Derby figures and Newhall cream jugs glinting in the sunlight on a cottage window-ledge. They are probably all underpriced, as well, for I doubt a customer has found him these last ten years or so. One of these days I'm going up into those Downs again . . .

One dealer I did manage to find, however, was Mr Young who did his dealing in an old water mill. But actually getting *into* his premises was another matter altogether. I passed his mill quite often. The millstream, drowsy with trout, chuckled its way over the weir into the pool and I often saw the equally drowsy Mr Young standing day-dreaming on the bridge in his little white apron as he took a break from the furniture restoring that was his speciality. He had restored the mill beautifully too and, because I had always imagined it to be stuffed from floor to ceiling with glowing old pieces of walnut furniture and dressers spread with Spode tureens and meat dishes, I had felt it was not quite the place for a humble dealer from the little cottage in the woods.

But one day I decided I would try to sell him what I thought was a fairly interesting set of six simple country chairs whose design owed something to Sheraton. They had tapering front legs and a squared style of back, the two horizontal rails very plain. The solid bowed seats were in elm and the rest of the chairs in fruitwood. They were a trifle wormed and a bit rickety, and so was the old lady I bought them from. I was able to offer her only £30 for them, for they were worth at that time only £60 a set in top condition, although now I suppose they would easily make £200 in auction. So I rang the bell-pull at the mill and soon the dapper form of old Young (if that doesn't sound Irish), covered in sawdust and looking just like the miller of ancient times, appeared from a side-door with a rather belligerent 'What do you want?' as he eyed my Transit in his drive.

I explained I had a set of chairs he might like and lifted the tailgate for him to peer inside.

'They need a bit of work, but I thought you'd be just the man for that,' I said hopefully.

'Good heavens, country Sheraton. Quite dreadful.'

But not so dreadful that he didn't ask, in the next breath, how much I wanted for them.

'About £45, I thought.'

At that, the mill-owner jumped spryly out of the back of the van muttering, 'They're not worth £10, young man. Good day.'

In an instant I thought that if that was the sort of price he was buying stuff in for, there might be some bargains in the mill, so I asked if I could come in and look around.

'Oh no,' he said, 'I wouldn't have anything for you here. Nothing at all. I sell only the finest English oak and walnut furniture. Good day to you,' for a second time. And with that he disappeared into the wheel-house.

I felt as humbled as a man who has just had a bag of flour tipped over him. Fearing that might be my actual fate unless I cleared off a bit smartly, I kept a weather eye on the top window as I drove off over the little bridge.

'Right,' I said to myself, 'the next Queen Anne bureau-bookcase I get in, I won't be offering it to you, sir.'

Of course, I have never had a Queen Anne bureau-bookcase to this day, any more than I have ever managed to set foot inside the Young emporium. I did go back there in an attempt to buy, some two years later, but I was only allowed into the bric-à-brac shed. And there was a set of country chairs, showing Sheraton influence, in elm and fruitwood and rather wormed. They were very similar to my set of a couple of years earlier – except for the price, £90!

What might be termed another eccentricity among country dealers is their apparent desire to offer cream teas and crumpets with the Chippendale. The Atkinsons, whom you have already met, served a very fine cold table on the lawns behind their shop in Canterbury. It was all most tastefully done with blue and white tea and dinner services in the Chinese style, the best cold meats from a local butcher and fresh cream slices that almost smiled at you through the raspberry jam. And all served by some delightful waitresses on summer vacation from college. The essence of summer contentment was to sell some nice porcelain to

Leslie and Ivy and then partake of their generous hospitality in a walled garden gaily flowered and visited by birds of many colours.

I can't, unfortunately, speak quite so highly of the culinary standards of another couple who dealt in antiques from an Elizabethan village house. The shop was full of cranky items such as Victorian bamboo hall stands, cutlery cleaners and moulting pheasants in glass cases. Not really my cup of tea. Nor, incidentally, was the tea-bagged brew and yesterday's doughnut which they served up in a cramped kitchen at the back. The pains in the chest I used to get after my regular trips to this particular establishment will make my first coronary seem like a holiday. But still, they bought quite a number of the cranky items I occasionally had myself, and at least the tea and doughnuts were free. I understand they got so carried away with the catering side that eventually they sold up the antiques business and went off to Dorset to manage a chain restaurant.

One way or another, what with the cock-fighting, the dealers you can't get to deal with, the indigestion, the cream cakes and crumpet, the mad dog and an Englishman who went out in the mid-day sun by his water-mill, life as a country antiques dealer could be pretty tough. Mind you, I went to an antiques shop in the London suburbs the other day: I found it with no trouble, the owners were a respectable couple selling an antique or two in retirement and their shop was full of the nicest things, all neat and nicely labelled. The trouble was, it was all so boring I just didn't buy a thing.

7
When My Boat Comes In

I can still hear the drip of rain on the roof of a Ford Transit van at midnight and the eerie sounds of the wood at Penrhyndeudraeth. There I was, huddled in a sleeping-bag on the floor of my van, unable to sleep because of the constant rustling of tree branches against the roof and the low moans emanating from the depths of this wild Welsh place. At first I thought the moans might be the mid-week rehearsal of some local male voice choir in a nearby village hall, but after a couple of hours of it I realised 'Land of Our Fathers' could never sound quite like that. Owls, vixens and the odd prowling badger were in fact the cause of my insomnia. So I brewed up the umpteenth Horlicks on my little calor-gas stove and prepared to spend a cold and rather frightening night in this dark copse.

I had set out that day for the Welsh coast near Portmadoc where some people, I was reliably informed, would sell me a boat. I had not quite made it before nightfall, so as one does not normally purchase a cabin-cruiser without first looking at it in daylight, I had selected what seemed a suitable place to park for the night. In blinding rain I had edged the Transit into the heart of a wood on a hillside near Penrh . . . (well, you know where I mean), brewed up a mug of tea to drink with eggs, bacon and fried bread and was now, at midnight, suffering the results of indigestion and an over-active imagination.

A friend of mine, John, who sold cars and other things from a bungalow in Kent, had by some means heard of the family in Wales with the boat for sale and had suggested that if I liked to go and fetch it and pay half the purchase price, we would resell it and split the profit. So, despite the fact that I had never before towed anything other than a Dinky toy behind the tricycle of my youth, I fixed a towbar on the Transit and set off for west Wales. Just because I was dealing in antiques I need not turn my nose up at a bit of cash from the boat business.

So here I was, cold and stiff on the floor of my van, dozing intermittently, if at all, and waiting for a dawn chorus I thought would never come. I would sleep fitfully for about an hour, then a gust of wind would send a multitude of rain-drops cascading down on the roof like a roll on a side-drum, whereupon I would remake my bed bad-temperedly and add yet another item of clothing to keep out the cold of a gruesome night in Gwynedd.

When the first blackbird of morning stuttered its oath from a thicket at dawn, I grumpily awoke to find myself covered in two sweaters, a pair of trousers, an anorak, a pile of furniture wraps and a teacloth. I lit the stove and felt better for coffee drunk standing amid the dewy grass and still-damp trees of a July morning that seemed a bit more like summer should.

Having breakfasted by seven, I climbed into the cab and set off with a little pencilled map given me by John to find the cart-track above the estuary that flowed into Tremadoc Bay and down which lived the family with the boat.

Three hours and about forty miles later, having driven round in ever-decreasing circles on the estuary side along country lanes that all looked the same, I discarded the map as useless and decided to ask at a farmhouse for the whereabouts of the cottage I was looking for. A man driving cows into a field pointed out the cart-track I needed, and to my disgust I noted that it lay through

a five-bar gate I had already passed at least three times but which I had thought led only to a disused barn. I took my frustration out on my willing V4 engine, and was soon approaching the cottage accompanied by three yapping dogs who, with wagging tails, ran neck and neck with the van on the last quarter-mile down the track.

If the welcome of the dogs was warm, the reception by the boat owners left a little to be desired.

'You the chap from Kent come to buy the boat?' asked Mr Thomas gruffly.

I informed him I was.

'Thought you were due yesterday,' said Mrs Thomas, slightly flushed.

I explained that I had arrived in the area late – it was a long journey from Kent – and had thought it best to look at the boat before I committed myself.

'Oh, there's nothing wrong with the boat,' said Mr Thomas, peevishly. 'John saw it a few weeks ago. I didn't think there was any doubt about you having it.'

'I don't think there is, either,' I replied, 'but anyway I'm here now and I'm sure we can do a deal.'

This seemed to reassure the Thomases and I was invited into the lounge. They indicated that I should sit on the Chesterfield while coffee was prepared.

Looking round the room, I noticed a number of antique furnishings and some nice items of eighteenth-century Chinese blue and white on a Welsh dresser next to the hearth. Obviously people of taste.

'Will you stay to lunch?' asked Mrs Thomas from the kitchen.

I said I would love to.

Soon the coffee arrived, and Mr Thomas started chatting about the new boat he was buying to replace the one I intended taking.

I did not pay too much attention – for two reasons. First, I was not much interested in boats, and second, because the smallest of the three friendly dogs, a Jack Russell, was demanding all my attention by leaping on to my lap and then bounding along the back of the Chesterfield. After I had made friends with it, it kept standing on the sofa-back and barking at a cat sitting on the ledge outside the lounge window. The excitement of the cat and me seemed to have an unfortunate effect on the animal – and on me – as it kept passing wind very close to my left ear and I was in the unfortunate situation of balancing a coffee cup on my lap, trying to look intelligently at Mr Thomas, while at the same time pretending that no, his dear little Nip wasn't annoying me in the least. Well, how can you accept someone's hospitality and then tell them their dog's farting up your nose!

I was relieved, in some ways, when roast lamb – Welsh, I suppose – and mint sauce appeared on the dining table and I had an excuse to sit somewhere else. But understandably the meal was not one I was able to enjoy greatly.

The social bits, for which I would not wish to sound ungrateful, being over with, I got round to the point of seeing the boat. Mr Thomas took me through the garden and on into a large, overgrown paddock next to a flintstone wall with a hand-gate. And there, in the field, next to the wall, and covered with tarpaulin, was the boat. It was, I suppose, about 20ft long, with flaking white paint, a broken rudder and was resting on a trailer with one flat tyre. She certainly looked very unprepossessing but, knowing nothing about boats, I was quite prepared to back John's judgment that she was a good buy.

'Is the tyre punctured?' I asked, concerned solely with my task of getting the thing home.

'Yes, but if we pump it up it should get you back, it's only a slow one,' said Mr Thomas.

'That's fine. The only other thing is, my van's in the lane and we've got to hitch the trailer on to the back. Shall I drive into the field?'

'Oh no, you can't do that. Neither your van nor the boat'll go through the gate.'

'It won't,' I said flatly. Then, risking appearing stupid, I said: 'Any ideas as to how we get the boat out of the field?'

'Same way she came in,' said Mr Thomas, confidently. 'Over the wall!'

'Over the wall?' I almost shouted. 'How do you get a 20ft boat over a flintstone wall, for goodness' sake?'

Silently I cursed John for not bothering to mention I might have a few hazards to overcome – like getting boats over walls.

84

Actually it would be very easy, Mr Thomas was going on. We would take the boat off the trailer, the trailer would go end-up through the gate, then we would place three planks up the wall this side, three planks down the wall the other side. I was to reverse the Transit up to the wall the other side, we would attach a tow-rope to the bow and stern and middle of the boat and gently pull her up one side with the van and then slide her down the other side by hand. Simple.

I scratched my head in amazement. 'Well, if you say so,' was all I could say. 'I'll go and get the van.'

Two in the afternoon on a July day which was now blazing with sunshine saw me, Mr and Mrs Thomas and three excited dogs puffing and panting in the field as we tried to slide the cabin cruiser over the thistles and on to the bottom of the three planks.

Every time we made a joint effort the vessel's lightest end, the bow, made greater progress towards the wall than the stern, and I fell in the thistles by a ditch amid clouds of dust from the parched earth. The dogs yapped at my ankles.

Picture the scene at 3pm: Mr Thomas was down to a tatty pair of ex-army drill shorts; three dogs dozed ill-temperedly in the shade of a clump of nettles; I lay on my back in the sun, beads of salty sweat trickling down my neck; and Mrs Thomas crouched over a tray of tea placed in the long grass, her skirt tucked into the tops of a pair of red knickers, her fat thighs blotched with nettle-rash, and all dignity gone. The boat lay on its side at the bottom of the planks.

'Better come and get refreshed, you boys,' said Mrs Thomas, and three dogs raised an ear each and then fell back in exhaustion. So saying, she placed a mug of tea between her ample thighs as she slumped on the field. Mr Thomas and I joined her as if at some macabre picnic, our bad temper being only slightly less hot than the sun.

'Looks like we'd better get Danny and Tot to help out,' said Mrs Thomas, chucking the tea leaves from her mug into the grass.

'You keep donkeys, then?' I asked sarcastically.

'The cheek of it,' laughed Mrs Thomas, in better humour with the tea. 'They're our neighbours, boyo. Always help out at times like this, don't they, Pop?'

'More a hindrance than help, I'd say.'

'That's mean, that is. You trot over and get them. I'll pour Mr Austen another cuppa.'

Grumbling, and with shoulder blades already growing pink with sunburn and thistle scratches, Mr Thomas shambled off in the direction of the lane. The dogs did not stir.

After two more cups of tea and an embarrassing number of glimpses at Mrs Thomas's frilly drawers, I saw help arriving in the shape of a dapper man in a charcoal suit, white shirt and tie, face as white as that of the recluse he must have been to be so unaffected by the sunshine. He was all of seven stone, with the pinched face of a man who spends his time studying fossils in a becurtained study. This, I presumed, was Danny. His wife, in wellingtons and a boiler suit and I know not what else, was by contrast red of cheek and ample of build, her pear shape bouncing across the field alongside the mincing figure of Danny.

'She's on her side,' said Mr Thomas to the newcomers.

'Yes, but let her enjoy her tea,' I said, meaning it as a joke.

'No, not my wife, the boat,' said Mr Thomas irritably, and without humour. He went on, 'Danny, you push her – the boat I mean,' looking daggers at me – 'at the stern end with me and Maude, and Tot, you go with Mr Austen to the bows. If we all shove together we should get her upright and settled nicely on the bottom of the planks.'

I was rather surprised that the woman had been asked to take on one end with only me to help. I was even more surprised when the man joined me at my allotted section of the boat.

'I thought Mr Thomas wanted Tot at this end,' I said, rather puzzled.

'That's right. I'm Tot,' said the man in a high-pitched voice which was matter-of-fact and completely lacking in humour. The men in these parts were a pretty grim lot.

If I was amazed at this apparent reversal of roles, I was even more surprised when, at the words 'All shove together now' from Mr Thomas, Tot gave all the signs of being anything but that when it came to strength. His suit still buttoned at the waist and not a trace of perspiration on his immaculate white brow, he leant into the fore section and, with little assistance from me and not a grunt from himself, pushed our end of the craft

86

perfectly into position at the base of the planks. Then, seeing the other three struggling with the stern, he moved to the other end and repeated the procedure.

'That should enable you to achieve the complete manoeuvre,' he said in his precise and rather sing-song voice. He brushed an imaginary speck of dust from his trousers and stood primly and alert next to the wall.

'Go and get the Transit into position, then,' said Mr Thomas.

I went to the drive by the cottage and drove the van through what passed for the Thomases' back garden and reversed as near as I could to the side of the wall opposite the waiting boat. By this time the ropes had been fixed to the fore, mid and aft sections of the vessel and Mrs Thomas chucked the free ends over the wall to me, her plump arms wobbling with the effort. I tied them all to my tow-bar, jumped back in the cab and stuck my head out of the driver's window.

'Ready when you say so,' I shouted.

'Righto, boy, off you go, but gently, gently,' said Mr Thomas.

I revved up and declutched slowly. There was a creaking sound from the other side of the wall and my wheels spun in a herbaceous border.

'It's no good, she won't grip,' I yelled. I let off the power and the van sank comfortably into the trench it had dug for itself under the rear wheels.

'Oh hell,' said Mrs Thomas. 'We had all this last time. Go and get the sacks, love.'

Mr Thomas did as he was asked and returned with an armful of fertiliser bags which he tucked under my rear wheels.

'Give her another try, then,' he said.

I again raced the engine, felt the rear wheels buzz against the earth and then grip on the sacking. The engine died to a low moan and the van moved slowly forward. I could hear from the other side of the wall the scrape of wood against wood as the cabin cruiser started to slide skywards.

'Hold it there, hold it there,' said a frantic voice from the gate as Mr and Mrs Thomas and Danny came racing round to my side. The Jack Russell followed at a rather lethargic trot, reluctant to miss any of the fun; and Tot followed, walking with dignity and a peeved look on his face.

87

'Right, we'll get on top of the wall and you continue to pull her slowly, like, till we steady her at the apex.'

I watched two of them scramble in ungainly fashion up the wall; Tot spotted an old Edwardian chair used for picking apples under a gnarled tree in a corner of the plot, placed it against the wall and climbed up like a man getting on to a train and with no more effort. I was beginning to admire the chap.

Again the van eased gently forward and I watched intently in the mirror as first the top of the cabin, then the deck and finally the hull lurched its way up the planks to be steadied atop the wall by two people who wobbled as they held it there, and one, Tot of course, who put out one elegant hand and firmly arrested progress on the part of the rudder which was still firmly fixed. Danny's assistance was no longer required.

'Keep her tensioned there,' Mr Thomas yelled at me against the throb of my semi-declutched engine.

The two atop the wall got down, solemnly lined up with the others at the bottom as though this were some kind of drill they had practised regularly for many months and at which they were now past masters, and it occurred to me that maybe that was precisely what *had* happened.

Not daring to look, I set the boat on her course down the planks, which had now been positioned on my side of the wall. My engine was racing and the Jack Russell added to the cacophony by barking lustily at my wheels and making half-hearted rushes at the front of the van.

The boat wobbled, lurched, there was a shriek of 'cut off the power' from Mr Thomas, the ropes slackened and the cabin cruiser tottered down the planks against the reverse thrust of three pairs of red, and one pair of white, hands. She was out of the field and into the garden.

'Righto, boys,' said Maude Thomas to men and woman alike, 'on to the trailer with her.'

And within minutes we had her loaded up on a trailer whose rather soft tyres shimmied sideways, to and fro, under the weight and shoving of our efforts.

Before you could say 'anchors aweigh', Danny and Tot strode and minced off through the garden without a backward glance and disappeared down the lane. No one said 'thanks' and no one said 'goodbye'. I felt awkward, but not wishing to upset things when they were going well, nor attempt to understand the quaint local customs, I simply turned to Mr Thomas and said, almost apologetically, which is indeed how I now felt, with all the effort:

'Er, any chance of trying her out in the bay before we finally decide?'

'Try her out, boy?'

And then an octave higher:

'Try her out, boy? Why, she won't stay afloat for five minutes!'

I felt anger rising within me, but frankly I did not have the energy to have a row. So I simply said, with an air of resignation which I hope conveyed my feelings on the whole incredible episode: 'Oh, it won't float. Silly question, I know, but I just thought, as it was a boat, that it wouldn't be impossible to expect it to do that!'

'Oh, no, she won't float,' went on Mr Thomas. 'Hasn't been in the water since a twelvemonth last summer. Her planks leak, you see.'

'But if her planks let in water and she won't float, surely there's not much point in buying her.'

'No, no that doesn't matter a bit,' he said peevishly, 'specially at the price we've agreed. John knows all about it. Why, goodness, man, she's not holed or anything. All you need is a bit of ship's tar and an afternoon's elbow grease to put her right.'

'You sure?'

'Sure? Course I'm sure. I used to have the same problem every spring, but you just patch her up and she's good for another season. Why, I've even got some spare tar if you want it. Come down to the barn and we'll have a look.'

So the pair of us trudged down the path to a large outbuilding, he with an air of thinking what a damn fool I was bothering about such things as boats that would not float, and I with a feeling that I was near losing my sanity. The sooner I could get back to the relative logic of Kentish people, the better.

But when we entered the barn, and as though a great cloud of depression had been magically wiped away, my frustration and tiredness suddenly vanished. For there – in the gloom – dusty and under wraps or else piled in little heaps, were all manner of antiques. There were corner cupboards, two grandfather clocks, a Vienna regulator, a Georgian pad-footed dining table, vintage car lamps under a bench, brass oil lamps on the window ledge and several pairs of coachlamps scattered around the floor.

My heart beat faster and I felt the start of a headache at the back of my neck. If only, I thought, if only I could buy some of this gear, then the whole ridiculous business with the boat would have been worth it after all.

'Think the tar's in this cupboard,' Mr Thomas was saying, rummaging through piles of old tools and beer bottles.

I continued gazing around me in almost total disbelief at the little Aladdin's cave I had stumbled on.

'Interesting old grandfather clock against the wall there,' I said, trying to appear to be only nonchalantly making conversation.

'Ugly old thing, I think,' said Mr Thomas. 'Can't stand old things myself. Nasty dusty stuff, antique furniture, and you tear your clothes on the nails. Give me G-Plan every time.'

'But your house is full of antiques,' I said.

'Came from Maude's family, all of them. Certain things the wife's fond of, so I put up with them. But all this stuff in here we can't stand.'

'Why don't you sell it, then?' I asked.

'Don't know, really. Suppose we've never got round to it.'

'I might be interested in a few bits and pieces if they're any good,' I said casually.

'From what you've been saying I should have thought you're not too keen on the boat now, let alone this old junk.'

'Oh no, I like old things. Particularly clocks. How much would you want for the old grandfathers?'

This was the crunch moment. Would he sell or wouldn't he?

'Longcase clocks fetch a lot of money now,' he said, rather shocking me with his use of the trade term for such timepieces. Perhaps he knew a thing or two, after all.

'Well,' I said, unenthusiastically, 'the ones with brass faces do, but these look like thirty hours' with painted dials. Nobody really wants them these days.'

'No one except you, it seems.' And, for the first time since we'd met, he actually smiled at me and added, with a wink: 'After a few bits on the cheap to help with the petrol, old son, well, we'll see what we can do. Offer me a fair price and you can have the lot as far as I'm concerned. I don't mind if Maude don't.'

I asked him what he'd call fair, up to my old trick of always getting the vendor to name a price.

'Well, we'd better see what's here first of all.'

So we went round the barn and made a list of the items to be cleared. There were two oak-cased grandfather clocks, both with 30-hour movements, one of them cut down, but perfectly solid Welsh country pieces; next came the Vienna regulator, which I wound up and heard going and chiming. Six mahogany corner cupboards, some with doors hanging loose but all there, emerged from amid the cobwebby corners; we located three pairs of antique brass and copper coachlamps and two vintage car lamps, also in brass; a school clock was nailed behind one of the barn doors; three copper vessels, black as a Welsh Bible, came to light under a workbench; a marquetry stationery box turned up in an old trunk, along with various items of decorative china, a leather hat box, a pile of old books and two brass oil lamps; and finally there was the dining table, c 1800, a bit wonky under the weight of a pile of fertiliser bags, but quite serviceable with a bit of attention.

'What would you like for the lot?' I asked after we'd both dusted off the grime and powdery animal feeding-stuffs.

'Hold on a bit and I'll get Maude,' replied Mr Thomas.

While he was away I did a quick assessment of what I could reasonably pay and leave a profit. I calculated the two longcase clocks at £60 each to the trade (this was in 1973); the Vienna regulator should fetch £45; the corner cupboards £25 to £30 each if they polished up nicely; the three pairs of coachlamps would bring £15 to £20 a pair; the vintage car lamps I didn't know about; the school clock would be worth about £15, depending on the movement, which I had not yet looked at; the copper vessels in the black would go for £10 each, £25 if cleaned; the dining table I guessed at £45, although I would have to look it up in *Lyle's* to be sure; and I allowed £25 for the other bits and pieces. That made a total of £475 at a minimum, even if I sold the lot to the trade and did not bother cleaning the brass and copper ware.

I awaited the arrival of Maude with some anxiety.

When she bustled into the barn with her husband, she said: 'You know some of these things are quite valuable now, Mr Austen; many of them are many hundreds of years old – they belonged to my great-grandparents.'

I did not feel like laboriously explaining that this would not make them *that* old. I simply said, as diffidently as I could manage: 'I suppose they might be if they were in good condition, but as you can see, the cupboards are tatty and have got woodworm and the brass and copper will take hours to clean, and time all costs money, doesn't it. I was mainly interested in the grandfather clock by the wall. What price have you got in mind?'

Maude looked at her husband, pursed her lips, and then said: 'We both thought £60 would be a fair price.'

'Oh,' I said quite truthfully, 'that would be too much for me, I'm afraid. That's top whack for grandfathers at the moment, so it wouldn't leave me anything for my trouble.'

'What!' said Maude. 'All that lot for £60. I know you'd have to clean it all up, but I'm sure you'd . . .'

'Oh, I thought you meant just the grandfather clock,' I interrupted. 'If you mean *everything* for £60, that does seem fair.'

'Well, that *is* what we meant,' said Maude, *her* voice a bit peeved now.

'In that case, it's a deal. I'll load up and pay you cash here and now.'

Hardly believing my luck, I trudged with the two of them up and down the path to the barn, loading each dusty item into the back of my van. When that was full, I locked the rear door, hitched up the boat on its trailer to the rear of the Transit and proceeded to place the two grandfather clocks and other items into the cabin. By the time I was ready to leave, the whole image was that of a rag and bone man who had come on good times.

I said my now rather more affectionate goodbyes to the Thomases, paid them £360 in crisp £20 notes (£300 was for the boat), selected first gear and creaked off up the track to the five-bar gate, and the roads for Kent. The three friendly dogs, lively now with the coolness of evening, barked and skipped and darted along the lane with me to the main road where, as my pace increased, they soon were left behind. I saw them stop in the road for an instant and then they turned, shook their coats and trotted back through the gate. Sentimentally I raised a hand to them in farewell.

Soon the van, trailer and all my goodies were bouncing and creaking along the main roads back to Kent, to which I drove through the night, scattering a few rabbits from the verges near Welshpool and a gaggle of late-night revellers in Hereford who gaped in amazement as my caravan passed by. And above the roar of the engine I sang 'Land of My Fathers' – with genuine feeling.

8
Eastern Promise

Among the many things I have kept from my days as a dealer, my collection of postcards I treasure as highly as anything. I acquired the bulk of them in a most curious way, but more of that later.

A few facts about postcards might help explain their fascination. Of course, the picture postcard is still very much with us today, busty birds at the seaside and views of the pier being as popular as ever. But somehow they lack the charm of the golden age of the postcard, largely a Victorian and Edwardian phenomenon.

It has been said that the inventor of picture postcards died in 1940 – for the fifth time! For at least five people have claimed to have devised them, including Ludwig Zrenner, Heinrich Lange, Cesare Bertanza, Alfons Adolph and Pastor Ludolph Parisius, who died in 1940. No one will ever know which of them was the genuine claimant, but we do know for sure that picture postcards were introduced in the latter half of the nineteenth century, with the very first coming on to the market in Austria on 1 October 1869.

British postcards were issued exactly one year later by the General Post Office. Printed by Messrs De la Rue, who still print stamps today, they were immediately successful. Half a million passed through St Martins Le Grand Post Office in London on the first day, and police were called in to control the large crowds everywhere that bought them on the first day of issue. I have a card issued during that first week in October 1870. This is a nice enough thing to have, but one bearing the first day postmark would now be worth over £200.

For two years the Post Office in Britain had a monopoly on the sale of postcards but in June 1872, after immense pressure to allow others to issue them, it became legal for anyone to print them, provided they conformed to certain regulations.

The first real *picture* postcard did not, however, evolve until later. The first authenticated one was posted in Heligoland on 5 August 1889, and shows coloured figures of a fisherman and fisherwoman standing either side of a coloured view of the island. The continentals had always been ahead of Britain in the development of cards and it was probably not until 1894 that the first British view cards were issued. There is still doubt over the date of their introduction but, for want of a better candidate, those issued in that year by Messrs George Stewart of

Edinburgh, showing small views of that city in the top left-hand corner, are widely held to be the British firsts.

However, before the turn of the century many firms were producing picture postcards in Britain, including Messrs Tuck, Valentine's of Dundee, the Pictorial Stationery Company and Corketts of Leicester.

By 1900 the craze to collect them, as well as simply send them, had grown apace. Patriotic fervour during the Boer War saw the annual sales in Britain reach the 500 million mark. It is little wonder, then, that so many have survived to give further delight to a new generation of collectors today.

No doubt they appeal to collectors because they reflect a world and a way of life now gone for ever; and because the quality of these penny pieces of frippery is often superb. One can but marvel at the beautiful photography on Judge's cards, the striking art nouveau designs of A. Asti, Raphael Kirchner and others, or be tickled pink – as the fat women at the seaside whom he depicted often were – by the comic postcards of Donald McGill.

My own collection includes hundreds of cards of Kent, and over 200 of Ashford, where I lived for a number of years. These I treasure, as they relate to places I have known, showing them peopled by a society with which I am unfamiliar. In places where I have stood stand Victorian and Edwardian folk with their quaint clothes and friendly demeanour, going about their business in a lifestyle that is now alien to us all. Life in urban areas now is so often brutalised and dehumanised, yet old postcards remind us of a Britain that still glowed in the reflected glories of the Empire, where men, women and children had time for one another and time, too, to enjoy in a gentle way the simpler things in life. Of course, I realise that beneath the surface there were problems and poverty and tragedy and death; those things have been with us always. But what seems to have gone is the unselfish interest we then had in one another, and in the world in which we dwelt; it was a less materialistic and self-seeking age I see in my postcards. Then was the era of true sentiment; now we must join the sex circus, have a bit of fun. The golden days of the picture postcard depict, alas, a vanishing world.

But indulging in such nostalgia has now become relatively expensive. I can remember in the early 1970s, when my days at Moses' sparked an interest in antiques, that a whole album of Edwardian postcards could be purchased for £2 to £3; to part with money for one single card would have been the height of crankiness. Yet now at the start of the 1980s, £2 to £3 each for cards is by no means uncommon.

Looking through *Picton's Priced Postcard Catalogue and Handbook* for 1979, I note that cards with designs by Arpad Basch, Maurice Denis and Louis Wain fetch anything from £10 to £30 each; that a postcard with an advertisement for Nestles milk on it is worth £8; cards showing horse-drawn fire-engines can be purchased for £6 each; that greetings cards for the Jewish New Year command £2.50 or those for Halloween £1; I see that cards depicting close-ups of village post offices are all worth over £1, and that those showing rolling stock on the Great Eastern Railway are available at £1.50 each. My cards with trams on are valued at £8 if close-ups or £1 if normal street scenes, and my postcards of cattle or cats a mere 10p.

Yet I can recall going to a house on Romney Marsh in 1976 to haggle with a lady who had a box full of albums containing cards in profusion depicting ships of all types from World War I. She had wanted £25 for the lot and I had hummed and hawed and told her I did not think I could make profit. So I had not bought them and had left in a huff. The minimum value of any one of those cards today, four years later, would be 50p, and in another four years' time, who can guess what. It is, indeed, a vanishing world.

But I did acquire a fine collection, very cheaply as it turned out, in a strange way. I was sitting in the study of my good friend and confidant Richard among the books, bathtubs, African carvings, U-bend pipes and other eccentric trappings in his possession. Richard's home has, over the years, been an enjoyable sanctuary for me, with his lovely wife, four beautiful daughters who have seduced me each in turn with their fey smiles and shapely legs; a collection of books and postcards into which I have often dipped pleasurably; and, of course, the great man himself, a worker in lead by profession – hence the accumulation of ephemera from the plumber's shop around his room – but a man of dreams and philosophy by inclination.

Over endless cups of Nescafe and the occasional bottle of whisky, drunk rashly, quickly and enjoyably with scant regard for the morrow, we have talked of lechery and ladies, Kant and constipation, religion and Rubens, high heels and hallucinations, *Penthouse* and the Pentateuch. Not, you will appreciate, necessarily in those pairings. But, like the walrus, we have found time to talk of many things. And when even talking had become dull, there were always the thousands of books and postcards which brought new horizons and delights.

Richard had spent many years, and not a few pounds, acquiring his cards, which ranged from an evocative selection of local topography through art cards of the era of Beardsley and William Morris to funny cards with small men with red noses admiring large women with red bottoms at the seaside. I would have put much money on the inseparability of Richard and his postcards. So you can imagine my surprise when, half-way through an evening's discussion on the relevance of hallucinogenic nutmeg to the study of eastern mystical religions, Richard dreamily turned to me and, apparently quite irrelevantly, said: 'You can have all my postcards. Just give me any sum you desire for them and they're all yours.'

I regarded Richard coolly for several seconds, assessing his state of mystic detachment, wondering if I could check his pulse rate without being rumbled, and finally questioning the advisability of getting his two eldest daughters in to assist me with him to the bedroom. But he continued to gaze at me with relative sanity – indicating one of his good nights – and the smoke from his Falcon pipe drifted reassuringly up to the ceiling. I detected strong emotions in the room and decided to play it straight.

'You must be joking,' was all I managed to say.

'No, I'm perfectly serious. There are only two conditions attached. The first is that Margaret (his wife) mustn't know, and the second is you must not ask why.'

I, too, resorted to tobacco.

While the place filled with smoke, like an opium den, I thought to myself: 'Margaret's short on the housekeeping again, or else one of the daughters is having a shotgun affair with the lad from the village and he needs quick cash for the reception.'

But I said: 'Supposing I only give you £1 for them?'

'That's fine with me. You give whatever you wish. And whatever you give I shall be happy with.'

I have known Richard long enough and well enough to realise that simple statements like that are not actually quite that simple. There had to be an angle here, maybe a philosophical one – yes, definitely a philosophical one. It was, maybe, a test of me: how generous would I be; or how mean could I become in my constant quest for goodies at the right price?

Richard continued puffing long and hard at his pipe, occasionally twisting his black beard into little curls at the side of his mouth. I remained silent while he shuffled off to the toilet and, typically, came back with his flies undone.

'You're flying low without a licence,' I said.

'Oh,' he said unselfconsciously, merely pulling his sweater down over the gap. And then:

'What's your decision, then?'

'I haven't made it yet.'

'It's quite simple. They're all yours, all the topographical lot, the comic ones, the art cards, my catalogues, everything. All you have to do is pay what you wish for them and then take them from the house this night and say no more about them.'

'And you won't tell me why?'

'I won't tell you why.'

'May I guess?'

'Guess away, but I shan't tell you if you're right. You couldn't possibly guess correctly, anyway.'

There was a dramatic silence, such as precedes important moments, for I had no doubt that, at least so far as Richard was concerned, this event was of quite some significance.

'All right. I've decided. I'll pay you £65 for the lot.'

Richard breathed in deeply, exhaled as a sigh, got up from his chair quickly, whereas normally it would have been a lazy heave to his feet, and began emptying the drawers of his secretaire.

I have not, to this day, decided what the sigh meant: whether it was relief that I had not paid a derisory £1; or shock that even £65 was so little for what he treasured so highly. I have never asked him.

He continued removing his treasures. Each little bundle was neatly and lovingly labelled under the correct category. Each town and village was put in a separate pile, and I was amazed at how wide a selection from the county there was.

I had, in a way, bid blind for the whole lot because, although I had viewed parts of the collection from time to time, I had never seen it in its entirety. And here, from two drawers, emerged a marvellous selection covering the county of Kent, superbly colourful art nouveau and greetings cards, glamorous ladies in their Edwardian glad-rags, old ships and trams, an envelope full of McGill and other comic selections, Louis Wain's famous series of cats, a bundle or two of pre-picture postcards and advertising cards, and a fat and rude selection of modern funnies with blonde tarts in bedrooms making lewd references to their pet pussies. In fact there were cards from almost every conceivable category.

In a sense, I felt rotten about taking them all. But the bargain had been struck, this was the way Richard wanted it, and there was no going back on the deal.

As I helped take the collection out to the car, I was amazed at how many cards it contained, and how good they were. It heightened my embarrassment at being forced to offer any price I liked: it seemed impossible to arrive at the right figure, no matter what I had said. A sum of £1,000 would have broken my bank, while one of £1 would, I thought, have broken Richard's heart.

But in fact he was apparently indifferent to the whole thing. He simply scooped up great armfuls of the collection and trotted out into the winter's night in his carpet slippers and dishevelled clothing to dump them all on the rear seat of my car. When the deed was done I felt like a thief who, in the quiet blackness of night, makes off with his spoils.

The collection loaded up, we sat down again in the study. Margaret, who had an uncanny way of producing coffee at moments of intensity in the treatings of Richard and me, came apprehensively through the door with a welcome tray of beverages. Warming her kitchen-reddened hands before the bars of the electric fire, she said:

'Everything all right, Richard?'

Richard remained silent, staring straight ahead at a print of Bosch's 'Garden of Earthly Delights'. The figures, convoluted in bestiality and other horrendous acts, seemed in some strange way to be a solace to him at his moment of grief.

'Yes, dear, everything's all right,' he said.

'Oh, good,' Margaret spoke quietly, sensing his mood, as she always did. 'I'll leave you to it, then, love of my life,' she said, and slipped away as quietly as she had come.

'I'll write out the cheque,' I said, because nothing else seemed very adequate.

Richard stared at the fire.

'I understand why,' I said.

He remained silent.

I gave him the cheque and he stuffed it into his pocket without looking at it.

My friend is a man of strong feelings. That a postcard collection could be so important may seem difficult to understand. I think he treasured them not for their intrinsic value, nor even totally for their charm. They had become to him, as had books and clocks and Christianity and, long ago, sensuous women before them, a kind of obsession. They fascinated him, and he had spent hours delving into the history of the subject, becoming entranced with streets full of old shops and urchins running errands, sweet children posing angelically with canaries in gilded cages, and fat ladies in striped swimsuits at Bognor. And I suspect that there had stirred within his complicated mind some notion that the Eastern ideology that he so admired was despising him for his obsession with earthly things; and that, as a gesture of supreme strength, he must renounce that which was dearest to his heart.

So he had, I think, decided that the supreme test must be taken: he must dispose of his cherished postcards and be indifferent to their going. I also believe that what I paid for them was genuinely of no interest to him: receiving little for them would not hurt, the pain would have come in the decision to part. What I paid was a test to *me*. Whether I passed or not I shall never know.

What I *am* certain of is that this gesture, melodramatic as it may seem to those not involved, was of great significance at the

101

time to Richard. So I made a little vow to myself that his cards would never be sold, that they must bring as much pleasure to others as they obviously had to him.

To this day I have every one of those postcards still, and I have added to them over the years. I have looked at them to delight myself, and for a considerable time they have appeared as a regular series in the county magazine, *Kent Life*, which has featured the many charming old Kentish towns and villages in the collection. The 200 or so cards showing the olden days in the area in which I did my antique dealing are my own personal pride and joy. One day, maybe, I will find a publisher willing to bring out a book, so that the fascination of my old postcards can bring pleasure to a still wider audience.

I hope Richard has felt rewarded for keeping his eastern promise.

9
A Nice Little 'Leggacy'

'My gawd, that was quick,' said the old lady as she let me into her little terraced house in Rochester. 'A dealer took the books and things away only this morning.'

'Well, my dear, I knew you were off to Australia next week and wished to be clear of your unwanted chattels – so I came as quickly as I could,' I replied.

Actually, I had shot round like a bat out of hell. In the antiques business you have to keep a good thing to yourself and act quickly. Robert had been contacted by Mrs Legg. She had some old books and atlases to sell and Robert had arrived hot-foot to buy some good eighteenth-century maps and an interesting leatherbound book or two. He had purchased a couple of other items as well but had only winked at me when I asked him what he had got. But he had generously offered me whatever I wanted to buy from among Mrs Legg's remaining items, he being content to limit his interests to books these days, plus, of course, the 'wink-wink' things I couldn't find out about. He had told me about Mrs Legg one morning, and by early afternoon I was round there knocking at her door.

'Oh, I see, you're the dealer's friend, are you?' she was saying as she led me into the little front parlour. 'Such a charming man, and he was so generous in what he paid me for the books and paintings.'

My ears pricked up. So Robert had been on to a good thing with paintings, had he?

'Good of you to let me look at the other items, ma'am,' I said. 'I take it that everything has to go before you sail for Australia.'

'The whole lot, dear boy. Come and look round, see if there's anything you're interested in, but do please leave me a pair of clean drawers for the journey out.'

'It's a fairly long trip, you know,' I said cheekily.

'I may be old, but I'm not incontinent,' she replied.

I smiled. We liked one another.

'Start in the front parlour,' she said, ushering me into a tiny room whose floor was bestrewn with packing cases, hat-boxes, piles of china and ornaments, a bundle of walking sticks, a mound of brassware, suitcases and a large collection of miniature bottles of just about every conceivable kind of

alcoholic beverage. For some reason, I ignored everything else and asked: 'Will you be taking the drinks with you?'

'Oh no, dear boy, there'll be plenty on the boat over, and anyway I only take gin these days.'

'Will you have one now, then?' I asked, making myself well at home by opening the cocktail cabinet and removing a bottle of Beefeater.

'How kind of you,' she said. 'I'll go and get a couple of glasses.'

Shortly she returned and said: 'Sorry, the glasses are all packed and I can't be bothered opening them up now. There's at least two bottles each in there. If you don't mind having a tipple like that, I don't. It saves the washing up, and at my time of life, dear boy, you've no idea what a chore that is.'

So saying, she uncorked her bottle of gin, raised it gaily to her lips and, with a wink as the goodly draught went down her throat, she said: 'Help yourself, but don't imagine you'll get me drunk, young man, I've been at this game too long for that.' She grinned, did a little dance-step and took off for the back room.

What an amazing character. When she had gone, I helped myself to a swig of whisky, which I much prefer, and as it raged down the back of my throat I sat on the floor and began to unpack.

The first suitcase contained a pair of Japanese Imari dishes wrapped in Christmas paper, while an adjacent box held an early twentieth-century bronze buddha ensconsed in the previous week's *Woman's Realm*. A Japanese eggshell tea service with one cup missing nestled in a shoe-box, while a battered suitcase contained a small oil painting of dogs and a Staffordshire teapot wrapped in an old pair of silk knickers that reeked of mothballs.

Soon a small bottle of Fockink caught my eye where it had rolled under the settee. Avoiding cracking any dubious jokes to myself, I read the label and discovered it was an orange curaçao brewed in Amsterdam. As I pulled the tiny cork, a delicious-smelling, oily liquid greeted my nostrils; lifting the miniature to my lips, I tossed back every sweet drop of it and chucked the bottle into the coal scuttle.

On with the unpacking: a bundle of postcards here, a silver cruet there, cotton vests in a paper bag; two standard lamps poked through the top of a Tesco carrier-bag, and I found some

105

sticky sherry glasses in an old shopping basket. They reeked of gin.

Gin. That seemed like a good idea, and I made for the cocktail cabinet again. This time my eye was taken by a label that said Elixir de Anvers, and I was soon swallowing a delicious nip of amber liqueur that slipped down even better than the Fockink. Tequila seemed a good chaser, so I uncorked a tot of Mexican hooch and winced a bit as it turned out only to *look* like water.

Back to the rummaging: a pair of late Dresden figurines, one in each of a pair of socks, and an Elkington of Sheffield plated platter and a silk nightie in a knitting bag.

Beginning to tire at the thought of unpacking further tea-chests crammed full of goodness knows what, I grabbed a bottle of Underberg from the enormous stock of miniatures and tottered through to the kitchen.

'All right to go upstairs?' I asked.

I was greeted by a snore from the corner, where Mrs Legg was blissfully dreaming sweet dreams in an armchair by the wireless, the gin bottle balanced precariously in an apron that drooped between her wiry legs. I crept out again and went upstairs.

A set of six 1920s oak dining chairs was laid across a bed in the front bedroom and a marble clock was tucked into a pillowcase on a bedside table. The dressing table, worth quite a bit as firewood, was covered in an evil-smelling mixture of hairnets and Outdoor Girl powder. I dabbed a bit on my shiny nose, pulled a face at myself in the mirror and drifted into the second bedroom, muttering 'It's the drink that's talking.'

Two photographs of an aesthetic-looking man, mounted in silver frames, rested on a tiny mantelpiece over an open fireplace with Art Nouveau tiles down either side. I wanted the tiles but only succeeded in breaking a fingernail on the putty, which proved immovable.

When I stood upright after examining the tiles, I had a giddy turn and pins and needles in my legs. Thinking I was about to have my first, rather early, coronary, I slumped on to the bed, dislodging the best part of a drawer full of buttons, two corsets and a Gideon Bible. They came to rest on the floorboards and I came to rest on a cotton pillowcase that barely disguised a rubber sheet tucked into the mattress. As I slipped into unconsciousness

I thought about incontinence again.

I came to with a start caused by a jug and basin set hitting the floor just as I lashed out at a drunken kangaroo that was jumping at me as I walked down Sydney high street. How long I had been dreaming I did not know, but at least it was still light.

Creeping sheepishly downstairs, I found Mrs Legg in the kitchen boiling a saucepan of water on a calor gas stove. It was five past three and I had been asleep all of ten minutes.

'I'm having afternoon tea, dear,' she said. 'Bit early for it, I know, but all that drinking's made me a bit peckish. I've just been reading the paper while you were dozing upstairs! Fancy a boiled egg and a cuppa?'

My stomach heaved, I felt the usual headache starting at the back of my neck and I said, 'No, thanks a lot, not the egg, but a cup of tea and a Phensic would be most welcome.'

'Phensic, dear boy, why, whatever's the matter? You've just had forty winks.'

'How did you know that?' I asked.

'Heard you shout out in a dream; it disturbed me reading the paper.'

'Woke you up from *your* sleep,' I felt like saying.

What I did say was: 'Sorry about that. I'm not usually a mid-afternoon drinker. Don't know how you manage it.'

'Well, if you're not able to have a little bit of what you fancy now and again, life's not worth living, I always say. And I've got a week or two on board the *Canberra* coming up, so I'm getting in training. I intend enjoying every bit of it, young man, every last drop. I may be going Down Under, but I don't intend going down under myself yet, if you see what I mean. Now, the water's boiling; boiled egg for you, or not?'

I shook my head.

'Very well, but you shall have your Phensics. Really, I don't know what you youngsters are made of, sleeping off a paltry glass or two of an afternoon. Why, when George and I went to the Savoy in the old days we'd think nothing of a bottle of wine each with the lunch, half a bottle of Courvoisier to follow and then drinks at the Salisbury at opening time before going on to Covent Garden.' Then, after a pause, she added, 'You don't believe me, do you?'

'Well, of course, you obviously can put a glass or two away,' I replied.

'No, not the drinks, young man, me going to the Savoy and the opera and mixing in West End circles with lords and ladies, and even a Buckingham Palace garden party once; there's an invitation to it in one of those boxes somewhere. Oh yes, my George was a distinguished man in his way. But not appreciated like he should have been. Not appreciated. And me neither. I was a lady once, you know.'

Drinking like that quite clearly meant she *was* a lady, I thought. But I did not say so.

By now, a little eggtimer nailed above the gas-stove indicated that Mrs Legg's three-minute egg was ready. Wrapping her right hand in her apron, she grasped the saucepan of boiling water, took a metal sieve down from a rack, poured the water from the saucepan through the sieve into a brown earthenware teapot, leaving a brown egg nestling in the metal mesh. The whole operation was done nimbly and with consummate skill, as though she had been doing this every afternoon of her life as a kind of exercise in dexterity.

Looking at my raised and expressive eyebrows, she said:

'Can't afford to waste heat the price it is these days, young man. The tea'll be fine, don't you worry; that water's boiled for three minutes. Goodness me, a day in the trenches is what some of the youngsters need today. Why, my George ate his boot once in the First World War, he got that hungry of a night.'

Then she smiled disarmingly at me, hummed a snatch of 'A Nightingale Sang in Berkeley Square' as she scuffled in a cupboard for an eggcup, and motioned me through into the back parlour.

'Yes, had some good times together, my George and I. One Phensic or two?' she asked as she poured my tea.

Beginning to like Mrs Legg a lot, I enjoyed my tea and listening to her reminiscences of gay parties and high fashion, memories of the lawns at Glyndebourne and the influential men her George had rubbed shoulders with during the last war. At that time, I took all these stories with a pinch of salt. Subsequent events were to make me change my mind.

Tea over, I asked if there was anything I hadn't seen. She said

108

there were a few bits and pieces in the kitchen, on tops of cupboards and things. She couldn't reach them as her joints were stiff.

I suggested it was all that gin giving her arthritis.

'Gin, young man. Gin be blowed! It's all the dancing I do at the Community Centre. Gin never hurt a fly.'

Suitably abashed, I looked for something to stand on. Finding an old mangle in the corner, with its split wooden rollers and big iron turning handle, I pushed it, on its rusty little wheels, under the cupboard. I climbed on to the small flat area that served as a worktop when the mangle was not being used for mangling, and groped in the dust and old newspapers on the top of the cupboard.

'If you find any packets of pound notes there, just hand them down,' said Mrs Legg. 'They were George's. He went a bit silly before he died – always hiding things away for a rainy day, he was; £180 I've found to date stashed away in the most unlikely spots. Thoughtful of him, though, wasn't it? He was a good man, George, a good man.'

'I'm sure he was,' I replied, coughing a bit on the dust I had just disturbed from the top of a box of wine glasses.

'Any good to you?' inquired Mrs Legg.

'Well, yes,' I said, 'if they're all in at the price.'

'We'll see,' she said.

Just as I was handing her down the box, the mangle worktop began creaking ominously, the pine plank of which it was constructed cracked, and I dropped six inches into the well above the rollers.

'Steady, boy,' said Mrs Legg, grabbing me round the knees with one arm, taking the box of glasses with her free hand.

As I could still reach the top of the cupboard, I continued handing things down to Mrs Legg, while she continued hugging me round the knees to give support while I swayed and stretched at odd angles. I found old teapots without lids, cups without handles, half a Staffordshire tea service hand painted with flowers in cartouches, and all manner of cutlery, as black as your hat, and all, unfortunately, marked EPNS.

When I had removed pretty well everything but the mouse droppings from the tops of all the kitchen cupboards, I clambered down from my unsteady perch and assessed what little treasures I had found. Apart from the Staffordshire service, a few good quality cut glasses and some plated cruets and things, there was not much of great value. In fact all of the accumulations of household goods and bric-à-brac throughout the house were not going to bring in a fortune individually; but the whole lot, with a bit of work cleaning things up and putting them in an appropriate auction or two, would return me a fair sum for my labours, so I decided to make an offer for the whole lot and sort the stuff out at leisure in the garden back home.

'Quite honestly, I can't give you a price for each item, Mrs Legg,' I said. 'Best thing to do is, if you agree, I'll offer you a sum for the whole lot except the bedroom and modern furniture, which the council will clear for you for nothing, and I'll take everything with me this afternoon so you'll be free of any further worries about it all.'

'That suits me fine, young man. How much are you going to pay me?'

I decided to try the price which uncannily kept coming up over and over again in my various dealings:

'I thought £65 would be fair to both of us,' I said.

'Fine. Can you get all the boxes into your car?'

So that was it. I could scarcely believe there would be none of the usual bargaining that goes on between dealers anxious to make a reasonable profit and owners of chattels who customarily have grossly inflated ideas of their worth. Mrs Legg was an intelligent and straightforward person, of whom I wish there were a few more in the world. I genuinely hoped the price I had offered would be a fair one to her, for really I had found it impossible to assess it all in such a short time.

Paying Mrs Legg from my pocket full of crumpled notes, I began the backbreaking task of loading all the cardboard boxes, carrier bags and old nightclothes and things stuffed with goodies into the back of my Cortina Estate. Being me, I shoved them all in without much regard for planning, and an hour later the car was groaning on its rear axle, the bonnet sticking jauntily into the air as though some monster were sitting in the back, and through the windows could be seen all manner of somewhat embarrassing bits and pieces, like dusty chamber pots and seamless stockings, a dressing gown draped over a box of Kilner jars, fire irons and walking sticks, suitcases and tea cups, a tin of oxtail soup and countless miniature bottles of alcohol rolling around under the front seat.

Grateful that it wasn't night-time that I would be driving this lot home through Kent – when I would surely be stopped and arrested by the first PC on the night shift looking for petty burglars – I finally managed to get the tailgate down as the last bit of old pelt was crammed into the back. I bade Mrs Legg a farewell of genuine affection, with best wishes for a long and happy time with her grandchildren in Australia. Perching myself uncomfortably in the three square feet of space left behind the driving wheel, I waved goodbye to Mrs Legg all the way down her road of little terraced houses before I swung on to the A2, homeward bound, my old car groaning and grumbling every mile of the way, for all the world like an ancient galleon creaking its way to the shipbreakers.

Over the ensuing days I made an inventory of the things I had bought, and in the weeks that followed I sold all the bits and pieces here and there, keeping a careful note of the prices realised until, firstly, I had got my money back and then, when I had sold all but one thing, had made a total profit of £145.

Mainly because I could see no market for it and partly because I thought I would have a good read some time, I retained a suitcase full of old letters and documents. I tucked it away in a cupboard at home for some months before, being at a loose end one afternoon, I decided to find out exactly what these old letters were all about. Thinking they would be the usual missives from children and neighbours in hospital, and such like, I was surprised to see, among what looked uncommonly like blueprints, a letter signed by the Lord Strabolgi, another, from the Air Ministry, to 'Monty', several communications bearing the crest of the House of Lords, another from Berkeley Square House, W1, signed 'Leathers' (Lord Ted Leathers? I wondered), and, at the bottom of the suitcase, a file marked 'Papers, patents, drawings, ideas, 1930–1945'.

Perusing some Air Ministry-Strabolgi correspondence, I was amazed to read of a proposal, submitted to the Ministry of Defence, to build a massive floating aerodrome, 150 yards wide and 1,000 yards long. Then, finding a blueprint for it, I noted that it had anti-aircraft defences all round the perimeter, a crew's galley, recreation and mess rooms, engines at the side to give steerage power, and an anti-torpedo 'blister' round the edges to ward off underwater attack.

As I sifted through the yards of correspondence relating to this invention, it became clear that George E. Legg, deceased, had dreamed up the whole astonishing scheme. He had, it appeared, been an Inventor Extraordinaire.

Immersing myself in the case full of documents, I unearthed details of some remarkable ideas. Apart from the floating aerodrome, Mr Legg had any number of other useful schemes to help Britain win World War II.

Pinned behind a complete technical and operations specification for the Browning machine gun, I found details of a retractable undercarriage to enable heavy tanks to operate on railway tracks, complete with blueprint. A letter to the War Office said:

'It is suggested that heavy tanks could be fitted with retractable axles carrying flanged wheels to fit our standard gauge railway tracks. The axles would be mounted on hydraulic rams, each axle having separate control and operated much on the principle of a modern hydraulic car jacking system .... It is hardly necessary to stress the advantages of a tank thus equipped, adding speed and mobility and the ability to leave and rejoin the railway at any point. If considered advantageous the width of wheel-base could be varied to suit any foreign gauge of track by the use of splined shafts and wheel-hubs which could be locked at any width ...'

Not content with his plan to make tanks more manoeuvrable on land, Legg next came up with the idea of floating them on water. Another document read:

'It is suggested that a float could be designed on the lines of the enclosed sketch, which would enable tanks to operate on water, in reasonably good weather, for the purpose of invasion, the said float to be powered by tank engines. This could be accomplished by providing a suitable extension and connection on the tank's gearbox, from which a flexible shaft would run to the propeller of the float .... Additional fuel tanks would enable a tank to operate for long periods on water, without using its own fuel supply, thus in an invasion it would land with full tanks . . . .'

Legg's inventive mind now fully occupied with resisting the dreaded Huns, he outlined a suggestion for a cable mine to be dropped from aircraft or laid by light naval craft.

'It is suggested,' he wrote, 'that it may be practical to drop mines from aircraft in the path of warships or other vessels . . . . The mines could be coupled together or, if this presents any difficulty, dropped singly with a small parachute of special construction which would have the dual purpose of uncoiling the cable and acting as a sea anchor in opposition to the mine at the other end of the cable. The cable would be supported by small floats at intervals with a suggested length of 500ft. The mine itself would float level with the surface of the water and could be designed to be self-destructive after a certain time or to sink by flooding of the buoyancy chamber . . . . The advantages of mines of this description would be, 1. The far greater chance of a ship striking them due to the length of cable; 2. The ability of a number of aircraft to ring a ship with mines and keep out of range of the very destructive fire from light "flak"; 3. As opposed to aerial bombing the damage caused is below the water-line; 4. If used as in bombing, the ability to straddle a ship with less chance of near misses.'

There was considerable correspondence about these ideas in the little brown suitcase, but whether the relevant ministries ever used the ideas I don't know. Probably I'm not supposed to know.

But Legg wasn't solely obsessed with the war effort; witness this application to the Patent Office:

'This invention relates to soap and is concerned with soap in bar, tablet or similar solid form. In connection with such soap, it is common practice for the name of the manufacturer or the Trade Mark of the manufacturer to be impressed in the surface of the bar or tablet during manufacture thereof and before this is dispatched to the customer so that when the soap is first used the name or other representation is readily visible to the user.'

Pointing out that the trade name appeared only on the surface of the soap, thus becoming washed away by the first application of the product, Legg says his invention could 'provide soap in bar, tablet or like form characterised in that [it] is formed in soap

113

of two or more different colours extending through the bar between opposite sides thereof and co-operating with one another in providing a design ... which remains continuously visible throughout the life of [the soap] until substantially used ... .'

That invention was dated 1 February 1950. Unfortunately for George Legg, a letter dated 28 March 1950, from none less than Lever Brothers & Unilever Ltd, pointed out that the invention 'does not show any novel features'.

A further suggestion in the patent application from Legg was for a method of saving soap by designing new bars with recesses so that small old bits of soap that were traditionally wasted could be stuck on to new bars.

With regard to this, Lever Brothers' letter said: 'The particular method proposed ... is not one we would wish to adopt.' You bet they wouldn't.

Perhaps having had trouble starting his car on cold mornings – and who hasn't? – Legg invented a heating device for internal combustion engines which, he told the Patent Office, would facilitate 'starting the engine from rest, for example, in the case of a road motor vehicle where the vehicle is parked in an open space under relatively cold weather conditions. The invention has for its object the provision of a heater applicable to the above purpose which may be adapted with particular ease to existing equipment of the engine.'

Legg's idea was for a heating element and burner to be fuelled from the vehicle's own fuel supply, so that a few seconds preheating would warm the motor nicely on cold and frosty mornings, enabling, he hoped, the engine to roar into life at a touch of the starter button. The correspondence held no clue as to any progress made, but from bitter experience I can testify that my car, at least, has no such refinements yet.

Having learnt, a month or two earlier, of the Leggs' liking for the odd evening out at the opera, I was interested to find the following among the correspondence:

'Having been a regular filmgoer for years, which means that my wife and self have been to the Cinema not less than three times a week, I would like to express my concern at the steady decline of the Cinematograph industry. This decline is in no

114

small measure due to the steady increase in Television, and with myself as an instance, I can say that since purchasing a Television set, I have not been to the Cinema more than once a week, and there must be thousands like me. This brings me to the point I wish to make, and I offer this suggestion for what it is worth and without much knowledge of the technical difficulties involved:

'Is it possible to carry Television signals by land line? If it is possible, then: Would it not be possible for your organisation to run a service similar to that operated by "Radiodiffusion", where instead of sound being carried over the wires, Films would be sent out. You would have your own station and everything would go out by land line, therefore your programme would not conflict with the BBC Television service .... Subscribers I am certain would be pleased to pay two guineas a year for the following services:

'A normal three hours Cinema programme not less than twice weekly .... The feature film should as far as possible be a "Premier" or first release, with a good supporting picture, plus the usual Newsreel etc. A children's programme could possibly be sent out early evenings ....

'If this scheme is at all possible it could be the salvation of our film industry. It would also be a boon to an entirely new public – the aged and sick who could never go to the Cinema anyway. Trusting this pipe dream will not have taken up too much of your valuable time ....'

It is not clear to whom our George sent his letter, but there is no doubt piped TV is big business today. Whether Mr Legg started the whole idea off I have no idea. But it brought back to me the words of his wife when she mentioned the lack of appreciation shown of him. I at least appreciate him and all the apparently good ideas of his I have tucked away in an old suitcase. I appreciated his friendly and humorous wife, too, in her little terraced house in Rochester, and it has never ceased to amaze me since what you can find stowed away in the most unlikely places. I sincerely hope she is still sipping a gin or two Down Under – in memory of the inventive genius of her husband. I drink to her, as does Robert, who did very well with the paintings, which came well up to Sotheby's estimates!

10
Valley of the Dolls

One night, when the Downs were full of rain and my heart full of despair at ever finding another bargain, I set off into the dank blackness bound for a nearby hamlet. It was the familiar Friday-night story: an ad in the *Kent Messenger* which might, or might not, prove a promising lead to some gear I could turn round at a profit. On this occasion, it was a lady offering a few dolls for sale – many, the ad said, in need of restoration. If that meant there were limbs missing and cracks in their porcelain heads, I would have to leave them well alone, for doll restoration is a specialist – and expensive – business. While there was always someone who would run up a new bonnet or a pair of bootees for me, sending dolls to a doll's hospital would tie up capital for many months.

However, I had had some previous successes with antique dolls and I actually rather liked them myself, particularly the Armand Marseilles, Heubach and SFBJ dolls I had handled before. These Continental, porcelain-headed dolls, so popular around the turn of the last century, were beautifully modelled, with cute, smiling faces and colourful costumes of the period. I can well understand the grip the collecting of such items has on many people – men as well as women. These particular makes found ready buyers in the trade at around £40 a time in 1976, and Ivy Atkinson at Canterbury was always in the market for perfect specimens to catch the eye in the window of her shop. It was mainly the German-made dolls that fetched that sort of money. French ones were a different proposition. Usually rarer and considered to be the finest available, they would sell for at least three times the price of their German equivalents.

The mid-70s saw a big boom in the popularity of antique dolls. The newspapers were full of ads saying 'lady collector will pay top prices for antique dolls'; or 'at least £50 each for any porcelain-headed doll paid by keen amateur collector'.

Collectors be blowed, most of them were dealers like myself, and while no doubt they occasionally did give £50 for a doll, you can bet it was a French one worth several times that amount. But the image of the amateur lady collector, with nice manners and a Volvo, seemed to do the trick, for I knew of several successful coups by such people buying whole collections on the cheap.

So it was not simply the blinding rain or my lack of a Volvo —

to say nothing about manners – that made me pessimistic about pulling off a deal that evening: I imagined that by the time I got there I would be following a string of dames in fur coats who would have snapped up the collection had it been any good. I had rung the advertiser as soon as the paper came out, obtained her address and been told not to arrive before 7pm. I reluctantly agreed, without giving away the fact that I was all that keen.

I secretly dreaded that most dishonest of all dealers – the Early Arriver. He is one who promises private vendors, as I had done, that he won't call until a certain day or before an agreed time, then drifts casually up to a house half an hour early claiming he has come a long way, misjudged the journey and would the lady of the house mind him coming in rather than sit outside in the car. Of course, the householder agrees, in he goes, beating the rest of the trade to the goods, and before you can say Armand Marseille he is pulling out a cheque book and the deal's been done. About half an hour later the vendor finds out from the next – time-conscious and considerate – dealer who arrives that the goods could have been sold for twice as much. And while you might think all this serves the vendor right for taking the first offer that comes along, I can assure you that any dealer worth his salt has a well-oiled and persuasive tongue when it comes to fooling private sellers into parting with a few goodies. Some of my own dealings, it has to be admitted, illustrate the point. On the other hand, I didn't think it served me right if, by observing good manners and adhering strictly to arrangements made with private vendors, I missed out.

So as my car sloshed its way through the sodden autumn leaves in the country lanes I was not, as I say, all that optimistic. After getting soaked to the skin climbing out of the car umpteen times to peer at strange house names nailed in trees or propped on country dustbins in the remote hamlets of the Downs, I finally found the old manor house I was seeking, nestling at the bottom of a rain-sodden valley

Parking on the verge, I negotiated a path through a muddy allotment that passed for the front garden, then slithered up some moss-strewn steps to an ancient front door with a rusty knocker. After I had hammered several times with my fist on the oak panels, the knocker being fossilised in its fittings, a dim light appeared in the depths of some distant corridor, and another bulb came on in the porch in which I stood, before expiring with a hissing sound. There was a pause, then footsteps approached down a stone hallway.

'We've lost the lights,' a woman's voice said from behind the oak door. 'And this door can't be opened – it hasn't been used for years; go round the back.'

With that she disappeared, carrying a flickering candle, and I was left to grope through the blackness to the rear of the house, stumbling into a gooseberry bush on the way and kicking over a dog's dinner placed right in the middle of the path to the back garden. Judging by the size of the repast, the animal must have been the stature of the Hound of the Baskervilles. I hoped the beast had left its dinner in favour of eating any Early Arrivers there might have been! My momentary amusement at the thought disappeared instantly as an alsatian tried to launch himself at me through the glass of the rear door.

'You'd better come in,' said a voice that emanated from a form about half the height of the dog and which was hidden behind the animal as it snarled at me through the window. The short, plump figure commanded the slavering carnivore to sit and opened the door for me. I walked in, slightly weak at the knees and not taking my eyes from the alsatian for an instant. Following the flickering candle, I was shown into an enormous kitchen that smelled of hen's eggs and paraffin.

'Let me just put a new fuse in and I'll be with you,' said the figure with the candle.

I stood by the glow of an Aga and watched carefully as Rinty, or whatever the creature was called, slunk past me and disappeared into a disused fireplace in the middle of the opposite wall.

Eventually there was a click and the room was flooded with light. A dumpy woman with large breasts that poked out of a summer dress that was too small for her turned to face me and said, 'You're the dealer who rang about my dolls, are you?'

'If I'm not, you're in trouble,' I joked.

'They're upstairs in a bedroom,' she replied, not bothering to smile, and looking for all the world as if she had taken me at my word. When she said she would follow *me* up the stairs, I could see I was off to a typically bad start. I suppose I must have one of those faces.

'Turn left off the landing and right into the first bedroom you come to,' said the woman. 'I'd better go downstairs and make sure the dog's locked in.'

Gone to fetch a shotgun, more like, I thought to myself.

I carried on into the room she'd indicated. Finding a switch just inside the door, I flicked on the light, received a mild shock, said 'ouch,' then received a bigger shock as I looked into the room.

There on an enormous four-poster bed lay about thirty dolls of all shapes and sizes, black ones, white ones, pink ones and some I couldn't see at all as they lay beneath tatty piles of mouldering blankets and other dusty debris. Some had no heads, others just an arm, and here and there in piles on an old eiderdown were legs, arms and heads, bonnets and bootees, eyes and wigs in hopeless, despairing disarray. It was like Vietnam after a napalm attack. I just couldn't believe it. And what was worse was the dreadful silence of the dolls. Just a still, dusty nothingness from among the disembodied heads that grinned back at me, the hands still raised in play, and plump legs that once were taken 'tatties' across a child's playroom. It was one of the most pathetic sights I've ever seen.

A minute or two passed before I could avert my gaze from the carnage. Sensing the woman re-entering the room, I put a formal, businesslike look on my face and turned to look at the owner of these orphans. I took in her lank hair and the look of emptiness on her face, the down-at-heel carpet slippers and the tights with holes in them. I noted again the fat breasts that wobbled in the restricting tattiness of a summer frock two sizes too small for her, and saw the streaks of grime that contrasted starkly with the whiteness of her flesh. She looked as sad and uncared for as the unwanted playthings of her bedroom.

Suddenly I regretted my silly joke in the kitchen, my attitude of joviality and optimism. This once-fine old house that now smelled of damp and decay, the menacing dog and the flickering candle in the stone corridor: they gave me a sense of being close to sadness and maybe tragedy. This was one deal I was going to play absolutely straight, with no jokes and no flippancy. I wanted to be out from all this, and quickly.

'They seem very damaged,' I said to the woman.

There was a pause before she replied, with a sigh: 'I can't help it. It's the way things are. I once . . . long ago . . . I once loved them. I dressed them all so beautifully and I brushed their hair. We had tea parties together, once . . . long ago. I used to sit them round the apple tree on summer days when the fruit was half formed and our garden here was full of loveliness and peace. And I made them sandwiches: cucumber and paste, and home-made raspberry jam; and we drank ginger beer, then sang nursery rhymes. Things were lovely here then . . . long ago . . . .'

She had a misty look in her eyes as she spoke. She stared straight ahead of her, with sagging shoulders, and in her dress she looked like a sad little girl, although I could picture her in the sunshine in that same dress, perhaps long ago.

'When David went I had to struggle. There was the house, you see, and the children were growing up. They needed clothes. Always they needed new clothes. So my other children – these (pointing to the bed) – they suffered. I couldn't dress them, as well. There have been no tea parties here for a long time now. Nearly five years. Sometimes as I can't love them, I've had to hurt them, so I've taken their arms off and not put them back; I've let them get dirty like this because they shouldn't expect me to treat them better than I can David's children.

'But they're all there somewhere, the arms, the legs, their eyes. I've thrown nothing away. But now they have to go, all of them. I cannot love them any more, my energy's gone.'

She sat on an old cane-seated chair next to the bed. I was conscious of my lips tightly compressed and a great sense of sadness at a woman made half mad by some tragedy I didn't like to ask about. All I would do was ask the price, pay and go.

'I need the money, too,' she was saying. 'There are things we must have. Now they can repay me for the years I cherished them.'

'How much do you want for them?' I asked.

'I need £200 and it must be cash and it must be tonight.'

'Very well; will you accept £100 in cash and the rest by cheque?'

'I'd prefer it all in cash.'

'That's all I have in money. I could get the rest tomorrow.'

'It's Saturday; no banks.'

'Oh, well, Monday then.'

'That's no good. Give me the hundred and an uncrossed cheque for the rest.'

So I made out the cheque by the bedside. I hadn't examined the dolls and had no idea whether what she said was true, whether everything was there or not and in what condition any of them were. I simply knew she needed the money and that I had to take a risk.

She said nothing when I counted out five £20 notes and gave her the cheque. She put the money in the tiny pocket of her dress, went into another bedroom and came back with an armful of cardboard boxes.

She then said: 'You must pack them all yourself. I cannot watch. Then go out by the door through which you entered. The dog won't be there.'

And with that she left the room and I heard her dumpy legs descending the stairs. There was the click of a door, then silence.

I could hear only the rain on the Kent peg-tiles as I walked back to the silent, broken children on the bed. I picked them up one by one and stuffed them and their dismembered limbs into the cardboard boxes like a greengrocer putting potatoes into a bag, and with as much feeling. I couldn't, at that moment, get involved with them. I had bought them and paid for them, but somehow they didn't seem mine. They were still part of this damp and ominous house. They had memories which I didn't share.

When the last loose arm and tuft of brunette curls had been tucked into the receptacles, I loaded the parcels into my arms and made my way down the stairs and out through the damp garden where the dolls had picnicked in the sunshine. It took two journeys along the flagstone corridors. On my final trip out through the kitchen I stopped to close the door, and from an upstairs room I'll swear I heard emerge the cry of a child from a distant place. It chilled me as it echoed through the still house. I ran across the allotment and hoped fervently that the engine would start.

It did. Driving off into the still blinding rain and the

blackness, I made my way back downhill from the apex of the Downs, and felt a great sense of relief at being away from that place. There had been the raw edge of madness there. 'When David went,' the woman had said. What had she meant: was David her husband, had he left her, had he died? It was a question to which I could never know the answer.

As I drove back, the rain eased and the street lights of a village shone into the car. Behind me in the boxes on the back seat, the dolls were rocking to the movement of the car. They jigged up and down and their little pink hands flapped and waved at me as we went over a level crossing. It was clear, in a way I shall never forget, that they were waving their thanks to me. Under their little hats, some still askew over their eyes, they were smiling at me, warming to my company and reacting to their outing like a charabanc of real children on the way to the seaside. I winked back at them, and said 'You're all right now, kids.'

When I got home I unpacked them all immediately and laid them out on my own four-poster bed, about which there is another story in the next chapter. There were, I think, thirty dolls in all, ranging from a few small bisque-headed dolls' house dolls, 6in high, c 1860, through some Armand Marseille and SFBJ specimens of about 1890, to a Heubach character doll of about 1900; there was a black baby of around 1940 and the most modern specimen was a composition doll whose glossy blonde wig and clothing dated her in the 1950s. I made a check on damage and found that just about the best doll, the French SFBJ, had her head smashed in three places. The pieces had been crudely glued together but I noted that the head was intact save for the tip of an ear. Very little, I imagined, could be done with her. A much smaller porcelain-headed doll of the late nineteenth century, marked 'Germany 8/0' alongside a Greek helmet — a mark I did not know — was intact save for a hair crack by the left ear. The chocolate-coloured baby was in perfect condition and so, surprisingly, were one or two others, but the rest all had limbs missing or heads with no bodies underneath. So I started sorting out all the odds and ends from the boxes and after a couple of hours' hard work and a few good guesses I had all the heads and limbs matched to bodies, although I didn't bother to adjust all the levers and bits of elastic inside so that they were actually fitted on. I surveyed the scene and was really very pleased that the deal had not proved so disastrous as the circumstances of their purchase might have indicated.

Then I had to decide what to do with them. This enormous gang of orphans on my bed – partially restored to health – seemed to be looking at me with apprehension tinged with gratitude. Although I had found all the necessary bits and pieces, I couldn't afford to keep my capital tied up for the many weeks – possibly months – that it would take to get them repaired and decently reclothed. Something had to be done with them now, *en masse*. Not for the first time in my career, I thought of Robert.

I went to the phone in the hall and called him up.

'Rob,' I said, 'got any good customers for dolls? Preferably handy with the Evostik and a needle.'

'Why, got some in stock?'

'Yes. Had a little deal this evening; well, quite a big deal, actually – about thirty of them, to be exact.'

'Oh. Where'd you get them?'

'Er, somewhere fairly local,' I said vaguely.

But Robert, who's pretty cute even on a bad day, simply said: 'I was going to go for them myself. The woman in the Downs, wasn't it; ad in the *Messenger*?'

'You could be right,' I said. 'Why didn't you go?'

'Had a meeting tonight; couldn't spare the time.'

'Well, you can still have them,' I went on.

'Oh,' he said, noncommittally, waiting for a price.

'But they'll need some work,' I said. 'You'll have to pass them on to your doll lady in Maidstone – the one who repairs.'

He asked the price – £300.

Silence at the other end. Then:

'Um, seems a lot if they're damaged.'

I assured him they were a good buy; there was plenty left in them at only £10 each.

'I'll have a look at them, then. Be over later.'

But not much later. It seemed about ten seconds passed before he was on my doorstep! Which was a bit smart, even for Robert, who normally bent over backwards not to seem too keen. Maybe that's where I learnt the technique. But he knew a good thing when he heard about it, and what's more I knew he knew!

'Phew, they are in a state,' he said.

And that made me smile at him, as his tactics often did. I knew his game, because I played it often enough myself: try either to show no interest or knock the goods a bit and maybe the price will come down.

Still grinning, I said: 'No, come on, Rob, no mucking about. You know they're worth it. There's a lot of money left in those for someone. But they need a good home: it was all a bit sad, the way I got them. You can be grateful, in a way, you didn't go yourself. I'll tell you about it sometime.'

For once, Robert didn't bother haggling with me.

'OK, I'll take a chance,' he said.

I gave him a look which I hope said: 'Pull the other one.'

So for the second time in one evening the strange family was loaded into cardboard boxes and piled into the back of a car. I knew Robert would sell them all again next day (for, I guessed, about £450), so that I had made £100 for my trouble and he half as much again for a bit more trouble, in the sense that he had invested more money than me. And neither of us begrudged the other a penny of our profits, for that is how the antiques business works.

As I helped Robert load up his car at about midnight, the rain had stopped and the sky had cleared. I saw that as a fitting end to a strange day. I kept the SFBJ, the German doll with the strange mark and the 1950s specimen. I suppose I took a fancy to them. They are sitting with me as I write this. They are still, alas, a little the worse for wear, but they remind me of the rainy day when I bought them. I keep them, I suppose, in case another sort of rainy day comes along.

* * * * * * * *

Jaunts into juvenilia have not always been tinged with sadness, nor the days filled with rain. I set off for a farm near Horsham, in Sussex, when the rhododendrons were drooping with lilac blooms and the woodlands twinkling at me with sunlight. A couple had answered an ad of mine in *Sussex Life* magazine for books and postcards relating to that county. They had told me on the phone there were some thirty volumes dating from about 1940 which they were prepared to part with. I always had a ready market for local topography, so the 150-odd mile round trip seemed worthwhile; indeed, on such a lovely day almost anything would have seemed worthwhile.

I found the Parsons' little farmstead down a lane where cockerels scratched in the summer dust and cows licked ecstatically at the moist elderberry leaves in the hedgerows. I was greeted by the inevitable little dog with whom I established instant friendship, and a cup of good country Nescafe, made with all milk, restored my vitality after the long, hot drive.

Mr and Mrs Parsons, slow of speech but quick to make me welcome, showed me into their lounge and soon I was examining the contents of a large bookshelf that ran along the entire length of one wall.

I soon hooked out the books on Sussex, noting there was nothing exciting but rather the more run-of-the-mill local history volumes that are the stock-in-trade of the village antiquarian bookseller. I reckoned to pay no more than £1 a volume for them. Inquiring if there were any more tomes they had no further use for, I was told the whole lot was for sale if I was interested, so I began running my eyes along the shelves for the sort of material that always sells well in the book trade: early children's books, natural history, travel, railways, hunting, good early literature, and so on. Not immediately seeing any of these, I examined a shelf full of John Buchan, almost his entire works, I thought, and decided to buy them for myself, to enjoy once again the delights of *Greenmantle* and be captivated for at least the fourth time by *The Thirty-Nine Steps*. Indicating that they interested me, I placed the volumes in a pile on the floor.

Borrowing a pair of stepladders, I commenced examining the top two shelves. An old leather-bound volume with loose boards came to hand and I was pleased to note this was an early edition of Cook's voyages – a bit tatty but guaranteed to sell. The next little goody proved to be a children's book illustrated by Edmund Dulac, one of the highly sought-after artists of the turn of the last century. Hoping it was an early edition, I placed it in the pile I wished to buy. Another leatherbound book came to hand – *The Complete Works of William Hogarth*, undated but with an introductory essay by James Hannay which, with one or two other clues, later enabled me to trace it in *Book Auction Records* (the antiquarian booksellers' bible); it proved to be a sought-after item, published about 1830. I was later to have it rebound in quarter calf and keep it for myself. Today it sits on one of *my* bookshelves.

And so the Horsham treasure-hunt continued. An old edition of Cicero's works I mentally put aside for my 'postcard' friend Richard, who I knew was sufficiently eccentric to get real joy out of this excruciatingly boring windbag. Cicero was followed by Thackeray, with a nicely-illustrated book on steeplechasing aptly bringing up the rear of the field. There were a number of other works I cannot now recall, but the pile I was intent on purchasing had grown to a fair height on the floor and I was feeling rather pleased at having gone. Deciding to have a last feel along the dusty top shelf before treating with the owners, I discovered a flat volume that had slid down behind the books on the shelf below. Blowing the grime off, I had a quick look inside and saw it was an exquisite scrapbook of the early days of this century. This was one thing I *really* wanted, not for its monetary value but for the superbly colourful bits and pieces of advertising ephemera stuck on its pages. I felt duty bound to mention this item, probably compiled by the Parsons' granny, which they had obviously forgotten all about, but was delighted to be told that it, too, could go.

Dismounting the stepladder, I came down to earth with a bump and hoped I would not do so again metaphorically when I inquired about the price being asked. There was no unpleasant shock: the Parsons wanted £50 for their little library. That was a sum over which I had no need to haggle, since it represented a good price for a number of items I could quickly dispose of in the trade. So I paid the Parsons cash on the nose, if you'll excuse the pun, and tootled off down the cart-track scattering a few irate cockerels and sending clouds of dust into the burning summer skies.

Back home, the first thing I did was to examine the scrapbook. I was not disappointed. On every page were laid out the gorgeously sentimental adverts for the household products of the early days of this century – many, I noted, still with us today. But how the marketing men have changed their tactics over the last eighty years. Nowadays a soap powder is likely to be

127

promoted on our TV screens by some effeminate berk prancing around a busy mum's kitchen tipping detergent into the Hotpoint and prattling on about under-stains and things being whiter than white. Around 1900 they had a plump black washerwoman standing on a lawn surrounded by what looked like a couple of acres of sheets and pillowcases drying in the sunshine. 'I'se middlin' proud,' she's saying. 'A morning's work.' That was the Sunlight Soap angle at the turn of the century.

There were obviously no taboos about being overweight seventy-odd years ago. Plumpness was indeed highly desirable, according to the slogan used by Shredded Wheat. Picturing two boys out playing in a snow-covered field, the thin one is asking the fat one: 'Hallo, Fatty! What do they feed you on?' To which the plump one replies, proudly: 'Shredded Wheat Biscuits.' Quite a comment, that, on the way society changes.

A belligerent bulldog guarding a table full of Fry's cocoa and chocolates does so in order that the copy writer can say the products are 'Unapproachable.' Cute it may be, but not the sort of psychology Fry's or anyone else would use today.

Nigger urchins and chocolate-coloured coons proliferate throughout the scrapbook, and you can imagine the uproar there would be today should such demeaning treatment and exploitation be attempted. Just sample this slogan for Cook's Lightning Soap:

'Five little nigger boys grinning in a row,
Watch Mummy Flannigan scrub Jim Crow.
Five little nigger boys screaming with delight,
Golly, Massa, Cook's Soap turns black white.'

That copy line, along with the drawing of five gawping black kids being scrubbed by a superior-looking white washerwoman, would be enough today to incite a Notting Hill riot, I should think.

Modern and rather sickening snob angles in the Sunday magazines are nothing new. In fact things were even worse in the old days. Take this as an example: A young lady in evening dress and carrying a fan gazes longingly into a ball-room full of upper class twits having a fraightfully good time under a chandelier. Inset is a smaller picture showing the same girl on the arm of an older man in evening dress, wearing monocle and white bow tie. The legend reads: 'My haughty sisters to the ball this evening go, their pride a fall shall have, I'll see them there and all their stuck up airs abolish ... She met a lord of high degree, who said: I never can love but thee! So now she lives in luxury, through Rising Sun Stove Polish!' Almost incomprehensible, and totally unbelievable.

There is an even more unbelievable ad for Koko. This one is endorsed by one of the great stars of the era, Ellen Terry. Above a heavily retouched head and shoulders picture of this celebrity runs the legend, ' "I use Koko for the hair." Miss Ellen Terry, our Great Actress, writes: "I have used Koko for the Hair for years, and can assure my friends that it stops the Hair from falling out, promotes its growth, eradicates Dandriff [sic], and is the most pleasant dressing imaginable." ' All that under a picture of Ellen with her hair sticking up like straw in a manner which today would provoke a chorus of 'Oh, oh, dry scalp!'

But although I laugh at the quaintness of an outmoded way of life, I am captivated by the delightful designs and superb colour printing of all the items in this scrapbook, which is a tribute to the industry of the child who compiled it, and testimony to the high standards of artwork in the advertising business all those decades ago. Copy writing was no more honest then than it is now, it seems, but because of its unbelievable naivety it gets away with it.

The Horsham Scrapbook has entranced everyone who has seen it. Whether hardened dealers or shorthand typists, they have all wanted to buy it from me: it has that little bit of magic. But though many temptations have been put my way, I have never parted with it and never will. I think that if it were reprinted today it would entrance even the modern generation of TV commercial addicts. Who knows, it might even encourage the children of today to throw away their Star Wars models and start a modern craze for the humble scrapbook. If they obtained as much pleasure from them as this big kid, that could be no bad thing.

11
Bedtime Story

It will already be clear that luck has played a great part in my antiques dealing career. Of course, most of the items I acquired had to be resold to earn me a living. But a few very remarkable bargain-basement lots deserve their own chapter and are special to me not just because of the price – which is amazing enough – but because I have two of the lots to this day in my home. Unless the burglars get them, I shall be very surprised if they ever leave it.

The first item I acquired through my habit of studying the small ads in the *Kent Messenger* on a Friday to see if there were any interesting items on offer privately in the neighbourhood. Well, this particular Friday afternoon I was lying on the bed after tea scanning the For Sale columns and trying to persuade a headache to go away, when I spotted an advertisement which was to result in me sleeping in a very different kind of bed that night.

'Old oak four-poster bed for sale in reasonable condition,' it said, quoting a phone number.

Leaping from the pillows and sending forty-seven Boots soluble aspirin tablets tumbling under the storage radiator, I looked at the clock and noted apprehensively that it was just after 5pm. I cursed myself for not looking in the paper earlier in the day, as I imagined that by now every dealer within fifty square miles would have been after an item that was as scarce as hens' teeth. And being an antique dealer is a highly-competitive business where it is the hares and not the tortoises that win the race. To use another metaphor, dealers remind me of a community of ants: they emerge energetically from their nests (the term 'heaps' could hardly be used – most dealers' homes are too well furnished for that) to swarm purposefully but quietly out over the surrounding countryside looking for a suitable carcase to pick over in the shape of somebody's attic or back parlour stuffed with granny's old goodies. Normally dealers are sensible enough not to sting one another — being, occasionally, too busy stinging the vendor — but they will use every devious tactic going to be first on the scene. It therefore seemed most unlikely the four-poster would still be available.

I rang the number, nevertheless, and was told by the lady who answered that it was still for sale and I could come out to see it straight away. Being realistic, I thought that meant one of two things: either it was not a 'right' piece, or else it was far too dear.

I neglected to ask the price, simply obtaining instructions as to where her home, Nooks Farm, might be. Saying 'yes' to every direction she gave me, I put the phone down and realised that, as usual, it had all gone in one ear and out the other. Following complicated instructions about how to find places has never been my forte. So I got out my Ordnance Survey map and found that, despite the intricate instructions given by Mrs Batt, Nooks Farm couldn't be simpler to find: it was about a mile away from where I had once lived.

So I raced off into the sunset still nervously imagining that there were a dozen or so other dealers bound for the same place at that very moment. I had often thought of devising a tippable box of sharp nails in the boot of my vehicle for just such chases as these, but I realised that, being me, if I did get up to such tricks I would only forget where I had pulled the lever, and catch myself out on my return journey! So I simply adopted the tactic of driving down the Kentish lanes at breakneck speeds knowing I would only be outstripped by those just the *other* side of sanity – or, once or twice, men in blue hats driving white V8 Rovers.

I was going so fast on this occasion that I actually shot straight past the entrance to Nooks Farm. I jammed on the brakes and the two wheels with a little bit of brake-pad left gripped quite nicely, sending me into a two-wheel skid into the verge. I went into reverse and then quickly forward again up the gravel drive, sending two moorhens and a muscovy duck with goitre to an early and irritable roost in the branches of an alder by the duck-pond. Quite to my amazement, there were no other dealers' vehicles in sight.

The lady of the house, either because of my noisy driving or the roosting cries of the waterfowl, was by this time standing apprehensively on the doorstep. I introduced myself and was taken into an old farm kitchen that had two wholemeal loaves and a plate of ham on a pine table, alongside a clutch of china eggs in a basket and a black labrador dog scoffing the remains of a teatime bowl of junket in the corner. It occurred to me that Mrs Batt was sharing too much food with the dog as, not to put too fine a point on it, if she had lost another couple of stone someone would likely have picked her up and smoked her!

Anxious to be on with the business in hand, she led me through the house up a creaky old staircase to one of the bedrooms. There, under the low-slung beams of a room partly shaded from the evening rays of the orange sun by a magnificent larch, sat a superb piece of old English oak. I could see straight away there was no danger of it not being 'right'. There was, however, one snag with the bed – the canopy was no longer there and the posts had been cut down. But it was such a lovely piece of wood I knew I must still have it. In colour it was the rich deep brown of a country gentleman's well polished shoes, and the panel at the head end was carved with a pair of serpents and a plaque which said 'E.M.J. 1700'.

It was clearly a marriage bed, made for 'E' and 'J' during the reign of William and Mary. It had been constructed and carved by a loving country craftsman for what I envisaged were a plump young rustic wench and her eager suitor. Closely examining this plain but appealing piece of history, I could see no signs of white edges – that, is, corners of the wood lighter in colour than the rest, where oak stain has become worn off a restored or faked-up item. For remember, when antique furniture was made it was brand new, and nobody in their right mind would have stained such a fine piece of oak. No, the colour on this piece was genuine right the way through.

Strangely enough, beside the bed was an oak chair which tried to kid me it was Cromwellian, although it was in fact one of the ruins that someone of much later date had mucked about a bit. On the chair, the oak stain was showing through all over the place, even though the wood itself was old.

Having examined the bed, I decided it was time to examine its owner to see what I would be up against when it came to haggling time. As I've indicated, she was rather on the lean side; in addition I noticed in the silvery sunlight cast on her by the sun shining through the larch, that she had a complexion like Dick Whittington's handkerchief. I hoped the acne and anorexia were not the result of sleeplessness caused by a bed less than comfortable!

'Well,' I said rather dubiously, 'the canopy's missing so I'm not really all that keen. How much do you want for it?'

'Is it?' she asked. 'I didn't know that. Well, I still want £100 for it.'

I screwed up my face in horror, at the same time thinking that it really was quite a bargain.

'Couldn't possibly,' I said. 'Not damaged like that.'

'Well, you can't have it for less. We paid nearly that for it in Lancaster twenty years ago.'

'Did it have the posts and canopy then?'

'No. That's exactly as we bought it.'

'I see,' I said, pretending to walk out of the room but actually working out the inflation rate. 'I can only pay that if there's a few bits and pieces you can throw in with it.'

'There's some duck eggs and lemon curd in the larder,' she said hopefully!

'I'm not really into the farm stall scene yet,' I replied. 'I was thinking more in the furniture or china line. I wouldn't know much about the market price for lemon curd.'

'Well, the Women's Institute sell it for 30 pence.'

'No, really, my dear, it has to be furniture. What about the oak chair next to the bed?'

'My Uncle Charlie made that,' she said, proudly.

'Oh, it's not old, then,' I said, playing innocent.

'Gracious me, no. He made it some time in the Sixties.'

'The *Nineteen*-Sixties?' I asked.

'Certainly. I'm not *that* old, you know.'

'Handy with the cabinet-maker's tools, was he, then?'

'I should say so. Brilliant, Uncle Charlie was. You come and see the dining table he made. It's down in the shed.'

So we trotted out into the garden and along the path to the shed, with me wondering why they couldn't eat in the kitchen like normal folk. Disturbing a few roosting chickens that were perched on the rim of a wheelbarrow in the corner, I spotted a box of books and a model of a Spanish galleon nestling among some flower pots.

'I quite like books,' I said.

'What sort?' she asked.

'Mainly the Marquis de Sade and Henry Miller,' I said wickedly.

'Yes, *Tropic of Cancer* was very good,' she said, calling my bluff and putting an end to any more of my jokes. 'But there's nothing like that in here — they're mainly children's annuals and things. I'd throw those in as well but I don't suppose you're interested in tame stuff like that.'

'Oh, I don't know,' I said, offhandedly, not letting on that children's annuals fetched a better price these days than anything that Miller wrote. In fact the market for that sort of stuff had declined quite dramatically since *Lady Chatterley* had become a coffee table book. 'OK, then, I'll take them if you like.'

'The boat could go as well,' she added, determined, now, to have her £100.

'Did Uncle Charlie make it?' I asked.

'No, I did, actually,' she replied, a trifle smugly.

'Not bad,' I said. 'Sure you don't want it?'

'No, the ducks attack it on the pond if I try to sail it.'

'Very well, that's a deal. But where's your uncle's table?'

Grabbing the ends of her skirt and swishing them into a corner of the shed, saying 'Shoo, Penelope, get down, Gladys,' Mrs Batt flushed a couple of broody fowl from an object covered in sacking, waited for the birds to run cackling through the shed door using whatever bad language is favoured by poultry, then whipped off the sacking and hen droppings to reveal Charlie's masterpiece. And I must admit it really wasn't bad at all. It was a small dining table with a centre leg on large, carved tripod feet, with the top smothered in very fine marquetry work. Small veneers in mahogany, oak, elm and walnut formed an elaborate pattern over the entire surface. A few squares were missing, and some had lifted with damp, but overall it was a most impressive piece of work.

Her uncle had made it about ten years ago, she said, but as she didn't like modern furniture she wouldn't have it in the house. It seemed pointless to remind her it was supposed to be a *Victorian* loo table!

'So I get the bed, the oak chair, the galleon, the box of books and your Uncle Charlie's table, and you receive £100. Is that the deal?'

'Well, as you don't want the lemon curd or the duck eggs, that's the best I can do.'

After pretending to think for a moment, I agreed.

The bed came apart in three pieces. The oak used in William and Mary's times turned out to be appallingly heavy. But thanks to my wife, ever ready to be a plumber's mate in such circumstances, the bed was eventually humped into the back of the Transit and taken back home.

Deciding it must be slept in that very night, we went into the bedroom to dismantle the divan we'd used since we were married. And there, spread over the eiderdown, was the blissfully recumbent figure of Sam the labrador, breathing slowly and dead to the world. I didn't like to mention to Joy about the forty-seven soluble aspirin tablets I had last seen lying round the storage radiator; as they were not there now, there seemed little point. But it certainly confirmed that labradors are the dustbins of the animal world!

'Food' and 'Walks' shouted several times into his ears eventually roused the dozing dog and after he had tottered rather shakily off into the kitchen in search of his supper we were able to bring in the four-poster. Thus it was that six hours after my post-tea nap I was stretching out in surprising comfort in a bed made for two young lovers 276 years beforehand.

You'll probably be thinking that at £100 it was a bargain already. In fact, it was to work out a good deal cheaper than that. I sold the box of books for £5 and put the galleon and oak chair into a little local auction sale. Nobody was really fooled by the chair, but I was quite pleased to see it bring in £15.92 after VAT and commission. The model ship returned me £8.50.

Encouraged, I spent a morning working on the table with some Araldite and a tin of dark stain antique wax polish. I reglued all the veneer that had lifted and replaced the little squares of marquetry which Mrs Batt had, thankfully, kept in a safe place. Then I wax-stained the whole thing and polished merrily away until it began to have some sort of patina and a resemblance to the piece of Victoriana it purported to be. When it was looking as good as I could make it, I entered it in another country auction sale and described it on the entry form as 'a marquetry loo table.' Which is exactly what it was.

The auctioneers, however, thought they knew better than me and described it as 'a *Victorian* loo table, c 1870, on centre pedestal on tripod feet, inlaid with marquetry in various woods.' Which was up to them, and as they disclaimed responsibility on their own and the owners' behalf about anything they offered for sale, it seemed it was no skin off anyone's nose, anyway. And it also fetched me a better price.

The table was eventually sold for £70.28, after commission and VAT, which meant the books, chair, boat and table had brought in £99.70, leaving me with a four-poster bed for 30p. That, you must agree, has to be one of the best bargains of the year.

Needless to say, with such a modest outlay I was able to keep it: I sleep in it to this day. Right in the centre of the bottom board there is a whole series of grooves and cracks in the wood where an unknown number of lovers have rested their toenails during their nocturnal capers. I like to think there might be opportunity to add a few more before I shuffle off to rest in the more permanent big bed in the sky!

* * * * * * * *

Mr Moses did not always have it all his own way in the market; every now and then the big livestock auctioneers in the town – majority shareholders, I believe, in this prosperous market – would decide to jump on the antiques bandwaggon themselves. Not with a great deal of style – simply by laying trays of china and brass, Georgian dumb waiters and sets of chairs in the stalls where an hour or two earlier they had sold a few dozen lorryloads of Romney Marsh sheep, some grunting sows and a bullock or two. They mucked the place out and laid some fresh straw as a gesture to what they saw as the slightly more fussy clients of the antiques world, but apart from that they treated a hogget or a Hepplewhite bureau in much the same manner. In the morning the auctioneers would wade through the muck in their wellingtons whacking their canes across the rumps of plump heifers, and in rough drawls that belied innate cunning and intimate knowledge of the equally fly ways of farmers, they would sell pen after pen of bellowing livestock. And in the afternoon the same auctioneers, with barely a change of boots, and certainly not of demeanour, would whip through 300 lots of pelt from the barns of the farmers of the Weald.

If you could put up with the hustle and bustle and the occasional nasty discovery under the litter, these sales could be well worth attending. On the particular day of which I write, there were a number of good quality items on view in the mangers and dusty outbuildings of the market complex: good quality Georgian and Victorian furniture, horse brasses, jewellery, a longcase clock or two and various miscellaneous lots, one of which particularly interested me.

On the floor between a Victorian chaise-longue and a couple of 1940s armchairs recently used by roosting turkeys, by the look of them, lay a cardboard box full of bric-à-brac. There was nothing much of interest until you scooped your way through the broken candlesticks and a gin trap or two. But at the bottom of the box, marked Lot 210, was a fine bronze Art Deco bust of a woman. The box of bric-à-brac itself was Lot 213, so the bust clearly did not go with it and had been cleverly concealed by someone hoping to get it for 50p or so along with the bric-à-brac. Deciding I could play that game too, I placed the bust back in the bottom of the box where I had found it and innocently moved off to another section of the sale. Checking the sale catalogue I saw that Lot 210 was simply listed as 'Metal bust of a lady'. But I knew bronze when I saw it and I had also spotted that this was a nicely modelled example of the Art Deco period; there was an indecipherable signature inside the nape of the neck. So I determined to buy it.

I hovered around the area before the sale commenced, just to see if anyone else would rummage around the bottom of the box. So far as I could tell, no one did.

With the sale under way, the auctioneer and his followers moved from stall to stall in brisk fashion, so that in less than two hours they were up to Lot 200 and moving inexorably in the direction of the bust. About Lot 202 I felt someone looking over my shoulder and turned to see Robert having a quick look down my marked catalogue. He asked me how much I was going to go on the bronze.

I said it didn't seem to be there.

'No,' said my friend, 'but I saw old Sid put it in the bottom of that box of bric-à-brac – Lot 213.'

'Yes, I found it there myself,' I said, instantly recalling the Sid to whom Robert referred. Sid was a shrewd weasel of a man with plenty of money and quite able to outbid the likes of me for anything he fancied at the sale. But for all his foxy cunning, I reckoned my friend and I could be more than a match for him.

'You think his game will be to get the box of bric-à-brac at any price?' I asked my pal.

'Probably, but it'll be interesting to see what the auctioneer does when he finds Lot 210 missing.'

'Well, whatever happens, you're interested?'

'Certainly.'

'OK, no sense in bidding against one another. Shall I bid on it and we'll split the cost and the profit?'

'By all means, but don't go mad. I'll see if I can fix Sid.'

'How'll you manage that?'

'You'll see,' said Robert, with a wink. 'From now on we don't know one another.'

And with that he moved off to find the gaggle of bidders who were following the auctioneer.

Before long, like a line of people doing the Hokey-Kokey without any music, the entourage arrived at Lot 209, the chaise longue.

'Righto,' said Les, the auctioneer, 'do I see a fiver?'

While Les was looking for his fiver, I was looking for Sid, to see if he was on hand to bid for the bust, which was due to be the next lot. There was no sign of him, which was puzzling, but Robert was there at the auctioneer's shoulder. I was pondering whether my pal had managed to trip up Sid adjacent to the muck waggon in the yard, but soon realised that would have been a useless tactic as Sid took little pride in his appearance at the best of times. And just as the thought crossed my mind, Les was knocking down the chaise-longue for £15.

Then, just as he announced 'Lot 210, the metal bust,' Sid appeared from nowhere at Les's shoulder, like a genie emerging from a bottle.

'All right, who's hidden the bust?' Les slanged the crowd.

'Can't find it, sir,' said the porter, a man more used to bullying heifers up ramps into cattle transporters than dealing with the devious devices of antique dealers.

'It's probably in the box of bric-à-brac, Lot 213; think I don't know a thing or two, do you?' said Les.

The porter rummaged, and found. He held Lot 210 triumphantly aloft.

'All right, you artful lot, now we've found it let's see some money for it. If it's worth hiding it must be worth a fortune. Thirty quid? Twenty? What 'a ya' got, then?'

'A pound,' said Sid.

'A pound!' screamed Les derisively. 'You go to all the trouble of hiding it, then offer me *a pound*! All right, you're mean as well. Do I see two?'

I nodded at the auctioneer.

Sid nodded at three, and I again at four. Someone else jumped in at five, and I went to six. Sid bid again at seven and I was back with it at eight. Just as Les whipped his eyes back on Sid from me for what he thought would be a nice little trot up to £30 to £40 between the two of us, I saw Robert turn to Sid with a doubting look on his face and I just heard him say the magic words, 'Careful, Sid, could be spelter.'

Les was impatiently looking at Sid. 'Do I see nine?'

Sidney opened his mouth to say 'yes', then he half turned to my pal and, with a look of doubt on his face now, I heard him whisper 'D'ya reckon?'

'All right, I haven't got all day,' said Les. 'Eight pounds I have. Going once, going twice. Gent with the beard.' Les scribbled irritably on his sale-sheet.

I had got it.

The funny thing was, Sid was now slyly gazing at me with a smug look on his face, as much as to say what a mug I was paying £8 for a spelter bust I would be lucky to get a fiver for, and wasn't he a right little smarty-pants for knowing a bad thing when he saw it.

For my part, I tried to hide my equally complacent grin at the way Sid had been outwitted. Robert, who knew Sid well, was aware of his two great weaknesses: first, to get stuff as cheaply as possible, and second, his even greater desire not to lose even £1 of his meanly earned cash. The word 'spelter' had been all that was necessary to sow the seed of doubt. He had only said it *could* be spelter, which was true, but for jack-of-all-trades Sid that had set the warning lights flashing.

Over a sausage roll and a cup of tea after the sale, my pal and I had a chuckle together about it all and agreed to put the bust into one of the better quality monthly evening sales some miles away.

So that's what I did. It was correctly described as a bronze bust of the Art Deco period and a London dealer bought it for £60. It was probably worth over £200 but, as mentioned before in this book, no dealer begrudges the next man up in the hierarchy making a profit as well. Possibly the modest price at the evening sale was because someone else had used the magic word 'spelter'. I don't know. Whatever happened, it was a fair enough return on an outlay of £8. Even old Sid himself would have been proud of a deal like that.

* * * * * * * *

Another occasion when the saleroom proved a good source of supply was at a quarterly quality sale held by another local firm of auctioneers who boasted that all their lots came from private sources. This particular time a substantial number of items arrived from a local family by the name of Pitt who included among their ancestors William Pitt the Elder and William Pitt the Younger, both former Prime Ministers of England. So naturally there were some good quality items on view. As I knew the furniture was going to fetch silly prices – my old rivals the Volvo owners came to this sale in profusion – I began looking in the nooks and crannies of the saleroom to see if there were any unconsidered trifles I might pick up at a reasonable price.

I'd noticed in the catalogue three lots described as 'two sketchbooks containing watercolours and other drawings', 'three ditto by Eliza Pitt' and 'four ditto by Eliza Pitt'. Finding them lying under a table spread with oil paintings and hunting prints, I opened them up. To my delight and excitement, they were superb. The biggest books contained many scores of watercolours painted in the Alps by an unknown artist but one who certainly knew what he was doing. The seven sketchbooks compiled by Eliza Pitt were almost as good. There were watercolours, wash and pen and ink sketches of delightful places in Britain and France drawn, I should guess by the costumes, somewhere around 1820–40. Whatever Eliza's relationship to the two famous Pitts, she deserved acclaim in her own right as an artist. For here were not the usual amateur daubs turned out by the leisured and monied classes of the period, but superbly crafted vignettes of the life and times in Britain and France in the early to mid-nineteenth century. The colours were delightful and the difficult medium of watercolour obviously fully understood.

Not daring to draw attention to these little discoveries of mine, I hastily thumbed through the albums before putting them back under the table and pretending they weren't there. I was eternally optimistic that I was the only one who spotted things under tables and at the bottoms of boxes. Unfortunately it was just as true this time as it had always been before that others were up to just as many tricks as I was. But I didn't know that then.

Mentally, I had marked these three lots down for £20 to £30 each which was what, if you were lucky, you could normally buy amateur albums of watercolours and sketches for.

Drifting past the porcelain counter, I bumped into a dealer friend, which was a bit unfortunate as he was examining a nice Vienna pot and cover at the time.

I thought the porter was about to need a speedy change of underwear as my friend Mendl juggled with the china before, thankfully, he replaced it on the glass counter-top. The porter swore to himself and put the Vienna back on the shelf with an air of impatience, as though we had reduced the whole serious business to the level of a coconut-shy.

Mendl and I exchanged a few pleasantries, said the usual things about there not being much about that was any good, that what was good would fetch silly prices and that we probably wouldn't come to the sale, anyway. Which was what everyone always said – without meaning a word of it.

'Got your eye on anything particular, Mendl?'

'The porcelain's nice but not exceptional. It'll fetch silly money, boy, silly money. How about you?'

'Not much here for me. There's a few drawings that are quite nice. Might have a go for them. We'll see.'

'The Eliza Pitt stuff, you mean?'

'Yes, those sketchbook things. Seen them?' I asked apprehensively.

'Seen them? I should say so – along with a few hundred other dealers.'

'The ones under the table? The books I mean – not the dealers!'

'Yes. There'll be a few score dealers with housemaid's knee tomorrow from what I've seen of them scrambling under that table.'

I experienced a sinking feeling. Mendl asked how much I was going to pay for them and I said about £40 to £50, already doubling the price in view of what he had said about the interest.

'Not a chance,' he said. 'I'd go to twice that myself. They're good quality, you know. But I wish you luck with them tomorrow,' said Mendl, bustling off to the silver counter.

Now, as if that was not bad enough, I saw Robert in the car park and it appeared that on the morrow, which was the day of the sale, he intended coming for a few choice books he had marked down – 'and for a few little sketchbooks I found under a table,' as he put it.

This was becoming ridiculous. It seemed that every man and his dog was coming to the sale just to buy these wretched sketchbooks which I thought no one had noticed under the table.

Fortunately for me, my usual air of optimism can, when the occasion arises, be matched by one of equal determination. And I was now bent on having some of those sketchbooks. Clearly, there was no question of getting them cheaply any more, so I simply determined to get into the Big Time and outbid any of the others – at any price. In my mind, I redoubled the price I would pay.

But overnight I had a better idea. On the morning of the sale, I spoke to Mendl and Robert and the three of us agreed that one of us would do the bidding for the sketchbooks and that if we got them we would split them up later. We were all quite good friends and trusted one another, so it seemed the most sensible thing to do. There was going to be enough competition from elsewhere without fighting each other.

On sale day, after the books had come up, Robert disappeared off home with a wink, and I sat next to Mendl in the crowded saleroom. The first lot we wanted was the two sketchbooks by an unknown artist. I waited for Bob, the auctioneer, to ask for the anticipated tenner to start with. I was all ready to help him out with a fiver.

'Do I see three hundred?' he asked.

Mendl coughed nervously and I nearly fell off my seat.

'Two hundred, then. Yes, two hundred I have.'

And off it went. Three hundred, four, five hundred, six.

'Count me out of this one,' I spluttered at Mendl, who was waving his hands all over the place. He was carried away with the excitement of it all, and if he could have used his legs for bidding as well, no doubt he would have. So there was Mendl bobbing up and down next to me as he joined in battle with a London dealer in the gangway. At £900 I heard him mutter, 'Bah, stuff it, it's madness,' which is what I had thought when it went above the hundred. From then on the London dealer and another battled on until the two sketchbooks were finally knocked down for £1,200. There was a respectful silence in the room, as there usually was at country sales when something fetched over £500. But the auctioneer, as confident and unflappable as ever, just went on with the next lot as though items put under tables fetched that sort of money every time.

And the next lot happened to be the three sketchbooks by Eliza Pitt.

'We obviously don't stand a chance on these, Mendl,' I whispered.

'Probably not,' he said – 'but I'm going to have a darn good try.'

'Well, don't try too hard,' I said, trying to remember what my bank balance was, and recalling it only too well.

'The Pitt watercolours,' said Bob. 'Do I see £20?'

Mendl and I both half leaped out of our chairs, he fluttering both arms as before and me nodding away like someone at a game of head tennis.

The auctioneer was up to £40 before I realised Mendl and I were bidding against one another. So I sat back and muttered to Mendl, 'All right, you get them, but don't forget I'm in for a half share.'

We nearly had them for £40, but someone else jumped in as the hammer was about to fall and eventually they were knocked down to Mendl for £80 – £27 a book, which was what I had initially thought of paying before I had realised that half the dealers in the region were after them. I couldn't believe my luck. But no sooner had the thought flashed through my mind than the next lot, the four volumes of Pitt drawings, was on offer. This time the bidding started at £40 and ended up somewhere between £200 and £300. There seemed no logic in all this: nine sketchbooks, with little to choose between any of them, fetch between £27 and £600 each. Lady Luck had simply smiled on me again, I realised.

There were some record prices at that particular sale and the £1,200 for the two sketchbooks was reported in the Press. Mendl and I simply chuckled together about this as, the following Sunday morning, we sat on the carpet of his lounge surrounded by several square yards of delightful little paintings which we had removed from the books and spread around the room. We decided the fairest thing to do was to take it in turns to pick the ones we wanted, going on until every drawing had been accounted for.

So, over a whisky or two, we gradually whittled away at the pile until every item had found a new owner. It worked out very well because Mendl had a fancy for the Continental scenes and I favoured the English ones. At the end of the lucky dip, I paid Mendl my £40 half-share and staggered out into Sunday lunchtime affected as much by the weight of the portfolio under my arm as by Mendl's generous measures with the whisky.

Later that week I kept faith with Robert by taking my little horde up to his shop where, in a back room over a Chinese take-away and a cup of tea, we went through the whole process again. The sweet and sour prawn balls were good, but these little drawings were becoming meat and drink to me in more ways than one. Robert generously declined to take his full half-share, settling for a few fine watercolours of Ramsgate and Margate for which he knew he could find ready buyers, plus one or two drawings for his own home. He in turn paid me the £20 which was his half-share of my half-share – and everyone was happy.

I ended up with two good watercolours of Hastings, a superb little painting of Conway Castle, an equally good one of St Vincent's Rock, Clifton, long before the suspension bridge was in existence, two delicately coloured scenes from Normandy, several views of north Devon and of Tenby in Wales, two delightful wash drawings of Kenilworth and Herstmonceux Castles, various other unidentified sketches and a watercolour of a Georgian house in a parkland setting. I had a number of them mounted, glazed and placed in Hogarth frames. The picture of the Georgian house I gave to Leslie and Ivy Atkinson as a retirement present, as it seemed to picture the lovely setting they chose for themselves when they moved to their home in Sussex, where the painting now hangs in their hall.

The framing exercise cost me £50 which, together with my initial outlay of £20, stood me in at £70 for this delightful little collection. I sold the two paintings of Hastings for £45 for the pair, and later a watercolour of Normandy fetched £25 in a sale. So now I am fortunate to have a selection of fine watercolours hanging on my walls which ended up costing me nothing. They remind me of the day I Pitted my wits – if you'll forgive the pun – against a battalion of buyers who also knew they had spotted something good tucked away under a saleroom table.

* * * * * * * *

Fortunate as I have been, I can still lie at night in the four-poster and dream of other treasures that are waiting to be discovered. I know they are there and, such is the romance of this antiques business, someone some day will buy them for a song and, like me, have a happy tale to tell. Maybe it will be you. In the final chapter of this book are a few thoughts that I hope will encourage and help you in your search.

12
Good Hunting

At the beginning of this book the point was made that the antiques game is not solely for the serious, the monied, the expert or the just plain lucky – although all those types of people are players within it, of course. But my experiences are sufficient evidence that its broad and fascinating compass gives nearly everyone the chance to compete with those who actually are serious, monied, expert and lucky.

Perhaps you have never had a great deal of success with antiques, much as you would like to – or you are tempted to get involved for the first time. If so, there are a few basic factors none of us can ignore and which I found out the hard, though enjoyable, way over the years. Here, then, are a few thoughts on what I consider to be essential points to bear in mind, whether you are dealing or dabbling, collecting or contemplating.

First, remember that there are not many genuine experts about. How can there be when you consider how many umpteen thousands of antiques and collectables there are? There are many successful dealers but few of them, unless they specialise, are experts in any one thing. So if you read as much as you can about antiques you can put yourself on a par with the majority of dealers.

Don't imagine for one moment that even the experts know it all. They can't: there is too much to know. I mentioned in the Foreword the Constable painting that slipped through a London saleroom for £38. The experts had seen it, and so had the specialist dealers, but that did not prevent someone realising the impossible dream. Believe it or not, that sort of thing happens regularly – not just with paintings, but with all the categories of collectables that exist. And if it happens in the cream of auction rooms, there is no telling what slips through the country auction houses in the course of a year. This is not to say that rural auctioneers are a bit dim: they're not. But in a weekly sale with maybe 300 to 400 lots, ranging from bedpans to a boudoir grand, it is impossible to expect that everything that comes under the hammer will have been expertly catalogued and sold for every last penny. So, with persistence, you could easily make a killing.

All the same, somewhere along the line you have to add knowledge to your line of attack. I would be the first one to admit that I had a lot of luck during my days as a dealer. Luck is no good, though, unless you cash in on it. I bought that Goss hop kiln for just £1, but by the time I got to Sotheby's with it I had armed myself with the knowledge that it was one of the rarest pieces of Goss around. That way I cashed in on it. If it had remained in the china cabinet at my cottage until a customer had bought it for the £7 I was asking, someone else would have written Chapter 2 of this book, not me.

Of course, if you buy in salerooms, whether they are in Belgravia or Bucks Hill Bottom, the chances are, if you are after something good, you will be up against The Ring. Now The Ring is a cartel of dealers who decide not to bid against one another in the sale, thus keeping prices down. They mutter darkly to one another in the car park on view days and agree among themselves that Fred will buy six choice lots and Joe will purchase five more at a mutually acceptable price. Because they don't bid against each other on the actual sale day Fred and Joe have to compete only against a few dabblers and a hopeful collector or two who have not the cash to give them much trouble. So the eleven best pieces are acquired at far below their true value. After the sale the members of the cartel disappear into the lounge bar of the local hostelry, there to have a second auction, among themselves, to decide who is going to have what. This is called the knock-out. The bidding for each of the eleven lots is started at the price paid in the saleroom earlier in the day, and the difference between that price and the sum finally reached at the knock-out goes into a kitty. When all eleven lots have been re-auctioned by the dealers among themselves, the kitty is shared out so that every member of the cartel gets a share. So you see even those dealers who go home without any goods after the knock-out still receive a handsome day's wages for doing nothing – literally. They simply had to keep quiet in the saleroom. All this is quite illegal, of course, but you will appreciate that there is very little the law can do about it. And there is very little you can do about it, either.

I competed against The Ring at most of the sales I went to. But as they generally went for the cream items, often costing over £1,000 each, I usually concentrated on the lesser pieces. If I thought they were getting something too cheaply I used to run them up on occasions, and no doubt they ran me up as well when they thought I was becoming a bit of a nuisance. This is not a game I would advise the newcomer to try, because if you are left having to put your money where your mouth is by The Ring it can be quite a costly business. I took part in this little war to let them know I was there. Over many months, my face became known to them and I was accepted as a fellow dealer and treated with a little respect. They never asked me to join The Ring but they did at least allow the occasional crumb to fall from their fat table.

One morning I remember an eighteenth-century Japanese crackleware vase coming up at a local quality sale. It was a beauty, apart from a chip in the neck: over 3ft high and nicely decorated. Nobody would start the bidding, so I cheekily offered a fiver. A member of The Ring trotted me up to £13 and then dropped out. So I acquired a magnificent piece of Oriental porcelain for a ridiculous price. I sold it that afternoon for £85, and no doubt now, because of the crack in its neck, it has had a fine shade and some electrics added and stands as a lamp in someone's gracious home at a cost, probably, of about £200. That was all The Ring allowed me from the porcelain and pottery that morning: all the subsequent lots reached a much more realistic price. The big boys had allowed me to win out once, and had shown what a powerful influence they have on prices. But if you can't beat The Ring – don't join 'em, just go for what they don't want. They are only after items that have a ready sale to the rest of the trade, so if your particular interest is antique farm equipment or something equally out of the way, they will not give you much trouble.

The other problem in salerooms and shops is fakes. There is a lot of money in art and antiques so it is very much a paying game to make copies of collectors' items. Furniture has always been copied. It is quite difficult to spot Victorian copies of seventeenth and early eighteenth-century oak furniture now, the fakes themselves having become antique. But if you know that, you simply view all old oak with a bit of scepticism. The problem is that the price of the humblest collectables has risen so much in the last decade that items that used to be cheap – Staffordshire figures and pot lids, for example – are now being made with a view to deceiving collectors. With so much money at stake, it is worth the fakers' trouble.

The only defence against all this is, once again, to arm yourself with knowledge. Read all you can about how the originals should look and feel, and then go and look at them at one of the hundreds of museums there are throughout the country, and feel them on view days in the best salerooms where it is pretty certain they are the real thing. Of course, you will still get caught now and again, as I was. Then all you can do is what I did – get rid of the thing as soon as possible and hope that you get your money back. But don't sell it to your friends. Put it back in another sale and hope to goodness someone else is as green as you were. Quite often they are.

Another way of buying is privately. If you are prepared to put up with such as the Wild Man of Romney Marsh, disturbed doll collectors in country houses and dustmen of dubious hospitality, there is much to be bought – at a price. And the price, as you have read, is not always monetary. Notwithstanding the vagaries of personality, most private vendors of old things know and care less about them than you do. So that puts you one up. Look at what they have to sell, assess its genuineness or otherwise and mentally note what you are prepared to pay for it. Always ask them first how much they want for the goods. That way, if they don't care much for them, you have got yourself a bargain. If they want you to make an offer (and that is what normally happens) play fair, offer them a sensible price and then – golden rule – SHUT UP.

You say something like, 'I can go to £50 for the lot'. You look them squarely in the eyes and then say no more. There will then be a silence. Often the silence will seem like a weekend in a monastery. But still you say nothing. And still you look at them. They will twist their apron strings – at least the women will, and some of the men I have met – and look at the dog, or their spouse, and then rather questioningly at you. But don't be tempted to say something like, 'Well, it's a fair price. I really don't think I could give any more'. In other words don't dither, just SHUT UP. It's a little psychological trick I learned many years ago. It nearly always works. More often than not you buy at your price – if you buy at all. Try it and see. Unfortunately, though, private vendors are a very fickle class of people. They agree to sell, then change their minds. They will get a price from you and then sell to the next dealer who comes along with £1 more. They will use you to obtain free valuations and they will barely apologise when their pet dog urinates over your shoes. So the occasional bargain you pick up will, believe me, have been well earned.

My own favourite method of buying is from other dealers. They are a friendly lot, on the whole, antique dealers. They share the problem of finding interesting things to sell and make a small profit on. Therefore, if you are one of them, you always get their sympathy. And if you are a collector, a dealer worth his salt will still give you a good buy. He wants you to come back again, after all. But the other great thing about buying from dealers brings me to my golden truth number two – there is a bargain for the taking in every single antique shop in the country. Yes, every one. There is always something disregarded or underpriced by the vendor. Underpriced either because he knows too little about it, or because he bought it for a song and, so long as he makes a modest profit, he is prepared to sell it for a song.

Of course, there is a snag in all this, as there always is. Armed with your knowledge, you have to find out what the bargain is. The dealer doesn't know (and if he did he would probably put the price up). And initially you don't know, either. You have roughly ten minutes to find it. Ten minutes is about the length of time you can expect a dealer's indulgence while you 'just look round'. If you try spending a morning in his shop every day for two weeks he will think you are either a VATman or a madman; either way he will probably refuse to sell you anything even if you do find his bargain.

When I refer to antique dealers, by the way, I mean the real professionals who, day in, day out, practise a skilled trade despite its hazards and vagaries. They are the salt of the earth. What I don't mean are junk shop dealers. What you find in junk shops is

151

junk. I never made a decent buy in any of them. The owners are as artful as a waggonload of monkeys and mean as the east wind across Romney Marsh. Any good stuff they do get in has already been sold to their regular trade buyers from the next town. They are fine if you want a plastic salt and pepper pot complete with congealed egg-yolk or a mattress with stains. You will get them both at a very reasonable price. But if, like me, you would rather live with your own muck, don't waste much time in junk shops.

When it comes to selling, you will find that if you are not greedy there is a ready outlet for anything old or interesting. The golden rule here is to buy right. Then you can always sell at a profit. Never, ever, try to diddle your friends or regular customers. If you have paid too much, either sell and cut your losses or, much better, keep the piece for a while until prices creep up and offer you a profit. If I could have back today all the stuff that has gone through my hands in the past ten years I would be wealthy, such is the escalation in prices.

Finally, a bit of philosophy: human nature being what it is, someone now and then is going to do the dirty on you; if you can resist it, don't do the same to them. If you do, you become what they are. And what they are is what you despise.

If my book has tempted you to get more involved with the antiques world, I can promise you it will get into your blood like nicotine. But as some practical help I have compiled an appendix of pretty well all the market towns in the British Isles, along with the local auctioneers. With this you can go out in search of your own Mr Moses and the local 'Tatty'. I haven't visited all these markets myself, of course: I looked them up in the local reference library. But no matter, I can guarantee that, armed with knowledge and lady luck at your right hand, you will find bargains galore. And I hope you do. Perhaps, above all, I wish you what I have had, a good deal – of fun.

Gazetteer of
Market Towns and Auctioneers in the
United Kingdom

ENGLAND

Avon

BATH
Market day Wednesdays
Local auctioneers: Aldridges Auction Galleries, 130/132 Walcot Street; Jolly's Auction Rooms of Bath, 1 Old King Street
BRISTOL
Market days Fridays and Saturdays
Local auctioneers: Taviner's of Bristol, Prewett Street, Redcliffe
KEYNSHAM
Market day Mondays
Local auctioneers: Cooper & Tanner, 8 High Street
THORNBURY
Market days Thursdays and Saturdays
Local auctioneers: H. E. F. Morris & Co, Oriel House

Bedfordshire

BEDFORD
Market day Saturdays
Local auctioneers: Peacock Auction Centre
BIGGLESWADE
Market day Saturdays
DUNSTABLE
Market days Wednesdays and Saturdays
LUTON
Market held Mondays to Saturdays inclusive
Local auctioneers: Bradshaw & Co, 9 Upper George Street
SHEFFORD
Market day Fridays

Berkshire

NEWBURY
Market days Thursdays and Saturdays
Local auctioneers: John D. Wood, 44 London Road
READING
Market day Saturday
Local auctioneers: V. & V. Chattel Auctioneers, 24 Greyfriars Road; Nicholas Fine Art Department, 13 Bridge Street, Caversham
SLOUGH
Market day Tuesdays
Local auctioneers: Buckland & Sons, 44 High Street
WINDSOR
Market day Saturdays
Local auctioneers: Buckland & Sons, 8 High Street
WOKINGHAM
Market day Fridays
Local auctioneers: Martin & Pole, 7 Broad Street

Buckinghamshire

AYLESBURY
Market days Wednesdays and Saturdays
Local auctioneers: Connell's, 2 Temple Street
BLETCHLEY
Market days Thursdays and Saturdays
BUCKINGHAM
Market days Tuesdays and Saturdays
HIGH WYCOMBE
Market days Fridays and Saturdays
Local auctioneers: David West & Partners, 5 Crendon Street

MAIDENHEAD
Market days Fridays and Saturdays
Local auctioneers: Pike, Smith
& Kemp, 22 Queen Street
PRINCES RISBOROUGH
Market day Saturdays
Local auctioneers: David West &
Partners, 9 High Street

Cambridgeshire

CAMBRIDGE
Market held every day Mondays to
Saturdays
Local auctioneers: Robert Arnold &
Partners, 55 Regent Street; Cheffins,
Grain & Chalk, 49–53 Regent Street
CHATTERIS
Market day Fridays
Local auctioneers: J. Collingwood &
Son, East Park Street
ELY
Market day Thursdays
Local auctioneers: George Comins &
Son, 3 Chequer Lane
HUNTINGDON
Market day Saturdays
Local auctioneers: L. Shaw & Son,
75 New Street, St Neots
MARCH
Market held Wednesdays to
Saturdays inclusive
Local auctioneers: Maxey & Son, 8a
Whitehart Buildings; J. Collingwood
& Son, Darthill Estate Office
PETERBOROUGH
Market days Wednesdays, Fridays
and Saturdays
Local auctioneers: Arthur E. Craig
& Co, Broadway Buildings; Lyall &
Co, 1 Queen Street
RAMSEY
Market day Saturdays
Local auctioneers: J. Jackson, The
Drill Hall, High Street
ST IVES
Market day Mondays
Local auctioneers: Phillip C.
Handley, Millerscroft,
Needingworth

ST NEOTS
Market day Thursdays
Local auctioneers: L. Shaw & Son,
75 New Street
WHITTLESEY
Market day Fridays
WISBECH
Market day Saturdays
Local auctioneers: Henry Bond &
Son, 8 Market Street

Cheshire

CHESTER
Under-cover market open Monday to
Saturday all day, but closes
Wednesday 1pm
Local auctioneers: Wright-Manley,
Sealand Estate; Sotheby, Beresford
Evans, 28 Watergate Row
CONGLETON
Market day Saturdays, plus
Wednesday afternoons
Local auctioneers: Whittaker &
Biggs, Moody Street
ELLESMERE PORT
Under-cover market open Tuesdays,
Fridays and Saturdays
Local auctioneers: Ellesmere Port
Sales & Auction Co, 38/40
Cambridge Road
KNUTSFORD
Market days Fridays and Saturdays
MACCLESFIELD
Market days Tuesdays, Fridays and
Saturdays
Local auctioneers: Brocklehursts,
King Edward Street
NANTWICH
Market Thursday mornings and all
day Saturdays
Local auctioneers: John A. Bee &
Co, 30 Hospital Street
NORTHWICH
Market days Tuesdays, Fridays and
Saturdays
Local auctioneers: J. P. Austin &
Son, Bull Ring
RUNCORN
Market days Tuesdays, Thursdays
and Saturdays

SANDBACH
Very large market every Thursday
Local auctioneers: Andrew Hilditch
& Son, The Square
WARRINGTON
Market open daily except Sundays
WIDNES
Market days Mondays, Fridays and
Saturdays
WILMSLOW
Market day Fridays
Local auctioneers: W. H. Robinson
& Co, 8 Grove Avenue
WINSFORD
Market day Saturdays
Local auctioneers: J. P. Austin &
Son, 9 Dene Drive

Cleveland

GUISBOROUGH
Market days Thursdays and
Saturdays
Local auctioneers: Saltburn
Saleroom, Diamond Street

Cornwall

BODMIN
Market day Saturdays
Local auctioneers: May, Whetter &
Grosse, 77 Fore Street
CAMBORNE
Market day Fridays
Local auctioneers: John Coad &
Son, Cattle Market, College Street
HELSTON
Market days Mondays and
Saturdays
Local auctioneers: John Coad &
Son, 10 Coinagehall Street
LAUNCESTON
Market days Tuesdays and
Saturdays
Local auctioneers: Kitton's, High
Street
LISKEARD
Market days Mondays and
Thursdays
Local auctioneers: Collings & Hicks,
Barras Street

LOSTWITHIEL
Market every other Thursday
PENZANCE
Market days Thursdays and
Saturdays
Local auctioneers: W. H. Lane &
Son, Central Auction Rooms,
Penzance
REDRUTH
Market day Fridays
Local auctioneers: Murdoch
Richards, Son, Alma Place
ST AUSTELL
Market day Tuesdays
Local auctioneers: May, Whetter &
Grosse, Tregonissey House
ST BLAZEY
Market day Saturdays
ST COLUMB
Market day Mondays
Local auctioneers: Trevail, Angilley
& Co, Fore Street
TRURO
Market day Wednesdays
Local auctioneers: Edgar Broad, 25
Pydar Street; W. H. Cornish, Castle
Mount
WADEBRIDGE
Market day Mondays
Local auctioneers: Button,
Menhenitt & Mutton Ltd, Belmond
Auction Rooms

County Durham

BARNARD CASTLE
Market day Wednesdays
Local auctioneers: A. & E. M.
Jackson, Newgate Salerooms
BISHOP AUCKLAND
Market days Thursdays and
Saturdays
Local auctioneers: G. H. Edkins &
Son, 122 Newgate Street
CHESTER-LE-STREET
Market days Tuesdays and Fridays
Local auctioneers: J. G. Usher &
Son, 15 Middle Chase; J. W. Wood &
Son, Bridge End
DARLINGTON
Market day Mondays

Local auctioneers: Addison Hudson, 105 Bondgate; Alan Ayers, 35 Prestgate

DURHAM
Market day Saturdays
Local auctioneers: Close & Weston, 36 Saddler Street

HARTLEPOOL
Market day Thursdays
Local auctioneers: John C. Leech, 123 York Road

Cumbria

ALSTON
Market day Saturdays

AMBLESIDE
Market day Wednesdays
Local auctioneers: Alfred Mossop & Co, Ambleside Auction Rooms, Compston Road

APPLEBY
Market day Saturdays
Local auctioneers: J. David King, 16 Boroughgate

BARROW-IN-FURNESS
Market days Wednesdays and Saturdays
Local auctioneers: Calvert & Beswick, 82 Cavendish Street; Lowden-Noall, 38/40 Cavendish Street

BRAMPTON
Market day Wednesdays
Local auctioneers: J. David King, 14 Front Street

BROUGHTON-IN-FURNESS
Market day Tuesdays

CARLISLE
Market days Wednesdays and Saturdays
Local auctioneers: J. David King, 12 Lowther Street

COCKERMOUTH
Market day Mondays
Local auctioneers: J. David King, 17 Station Street

EGREMONT
Market day Fridays
Local auctioneers: H. Kirkby, Crakesdale, Blackling

KENDAL
Market days Wednesdays and Saturdays
Local auctioneers: K. & D.'s Auction Mart, 10 Kent Street

KESWICK
Market day Saturdays
Local auctioneers: J. David King, 14 St John's Street

KIRKBY LONSDALE
Market day Thursdays
Local auctioneers: M. B. Hodgson & Son, 44 Main Street

KIRKBY STEPHEN
Market day Mondays
Local auctioneers: Penrith Farmer's & Kidd's Ltd, The Delves, Winton

MARYPORT
Market day Fridays
Local auctioneers: Thomson, Roddick & Laurie, 18 Curzon Street

MILNTHORPE
Market day Fridays

PENRITH
Market days Tuesdays and Saturdays
Local auctioneers: J. David King, 49 King Street

SEDBERGH
Market day Wednesdays
Local auctioneers: Sedbergh Auction Mart

SHAP
Market day Mondays

SILLOTH
Market day Fridays

ULVERSTON
Market days Thursdays and Saturdays
Local auctioneers: Lowden-Noall, 2 Market Street

WHITEHAVEN
Market days Wednesdays and Saturdays
Local auctioneers: J. David King, 76 Lowther Street

WIGTON
Market day Tuesdays
Local auctioneers: Thomson, Roddick & Laurie, 26 King Street

WORKINGTON
Market days Wednesdays and Saturdays
Local auctioneers: J. David King, 19 Oxford Street

Derbyshire

ALFRETON
Market days Fridays and Saturdays
Local auctioneers: Lee, Son & Coupe, 80 High Street
ASHBOURNE
Market days Thursdays and Saturdays
BAKEWELL
Market day Mondays
Local auctioneers: John Smallman & Co, Rutland Square
BELPER
Market day Saturdays
BOLSOVER
Market day Fridays
BUXTON
Market day Saturdays
CHAPEL-EN-LE-FRITH
Market day Thursdays
Local auctioneers: T. J. J. Weaving & Son, 17 Market Street
CHESTERFIELD
Market days Mondays, Fridays and Saturdays
Local auctioneers: W. T. Parker, 5 Vicar Lane
DERBY
Market held in Market Hall every day from Mondays to Saturdays inclusive; at Allenton on Fridays and Saturdays; and at the Eagle Centre on Tuesdays, Thursdays, Fridays and Saturdays
Local auctioneers: Allen & Farquhar, 30 Market Place; Richardson & Linnell, St James's Street
ECKINGTON
Market days Mondays, Tuesdays and Fridays
GLOSSOP
Market days Fridays and Saturdays

HEANOR
Market days Fridays and Saturdays
ILKESTON
Market days Thursdays and Saturdays
Local auctioneers: Theobalds Beardsley, 22 South Street
LONG EATON
Market days Fridays and Saturdays
Local auctioneers: Frank Innes, 61 Market Place
MATLOCK
Market days Tuesdays and Fridays
Local auctioneers: Robert E. Spark & Co, Matlock Auction Gallery, Oxford House, 31 Dale Road
NEW MILLS
Market days Fridays and Saturdays
RIPLEY
Market days Fridays and Saturdays
SHIREBROOK
Market day Fridays
Local auctioneers: W. & F. C. Bonham & Sons, Langwith Mill House, Nether Langwith
STAVELEY
Market day Fridays
SWADLINCOTE
Market days Fridays and Saturdays
WIRKSWORTH
Market day Tuesdays

Devon

ASHBURTON
Market day first Thursday every month
Local auctioneers: Rendell's, Old Mill Brewery, Stone Park
AXMINSTER
Market day Thursdays
Local auctioneers: Bonham's, Coaxdon Hall
BARNSTAPLE
Market days Tuesdays and Fridays
Local auctioneers: Fox & Sons, 1 Bear Street; Phillips & Sanders, 4 Cross Street

BIDEFORD
Market days Tuesdays and
Saturdays
Local auctioneers: Kivell & Sons, 4
Bridgeland Street

DARTMOUTH
Market days Tuesdays and
Saturdays
Local auctioneers: Letcher & Scorer,
9 South Embankment

EXETER
Market days Mondays and Fridays
Local auctioneers: T. A. Connole, 9
Queens Road; Phillips & Hussey's,
Alphin Brook Road, Alphington

HOLSWORTHY
Market days Wednesdays and
Thursdays
Local auctioneers: Kivell & Sons, 12
The Square

HONITON
Market days Tuesdays and
Saturdays
Local auctioneers: Redfern &
Plimmer, 105 High Street; T. D.
Hussey & Son, 99 High Street

ILFRACOMBE
Market day Saturdays
Local auctioneers: John C. Webber
& Son, 48 High Street

KINGSBRIDGE
Market day Wednesdays
Local auctioneers: G. M. Tompkins,
105 Fore Street; Luscombe, May &
Co, 62 Fore Street

NEWTON ABBOT
Market days Wednesdays and
Saturdays
Local auctioneers: Keith McCallum
& Son, 3 Union Street

OKEHAMPTON
Market day Saturdays
Local auctioneers: Mid-Devon
Auctions, 11 St James Street

PLYMOUTH
Market every day Mondays to
Saturdays
Local auctioneers: Arthur Abbiss &
Co, 6 North Road East; Constable &
Son, 2 Queen Anne Terrace, North
Hill

SOUTH MOLTON
Market day Thursdays
Local auctioneers: John C. Webber
& Son, The Square

TAVISTOCK
Market days Wednesdays and
Fridays
Local auctioneers: Kivell & Sons, 3
Brook Street

TIVERTON
Market days Tuesdays and
Saturdays
Local auctioneers: Fox & Sons, 5
Fore Street

TORRINGTON
Market days Thursdays and
Saturdays
Local auctioneers: North Devon
Auctions, The Square

TOTNES
Market days Tuesdays and Fridays
Local auctioneers: Peter Breton,
34 Fore Street

Dorset

BLANDFORD
Market days Thursdays and
Saturdays
Local auctioneers: Alfred Briskell &
Co, 1a Alfred Street

BRIDPORT
Market days Wednesdays and
Saturdays
Local auctioneers: Humbert's, 59
East Street

CHRISTCHURCH
Market day Mondays
Local auctioneers: Bulstrode's,
Stour Road

DORCHESTER
Market days Wednesdays and
Saturdays
Local auctioneers: Hy. Duke & Son,
40 South Street

SHAFTESBURY
Market day Thursdays
Local auctioneers: Humbert's, 34
High Street; John Jeffrey
Auctioneers, The Commons

SHERBORNE
Market day Thursdays
Local auctioneers: Palmer Snell, 65
Cheap Street
WAREHAM
Market day Thursdays
Local auctioneers: Miles & Son, 10
West Street
WEYMOUTH
Market day (at Westham) Thursdays
Local auctioneers: The Nutshell,
9 Ranelagh Road
WIMBORNE MINSTER
Market days Tuesdays and Fridays
Local auctioneers: Tweedale &
Riley, 51 High Street

East Sussex

BATTLE
Market day Fridays
Local auctioneers: Burstow &
Hewett, 12 and 13 High Street
BEXHILL
Market day Thursdays
Local auctioneers: Fryers Auction
Rooms, Amherst Road
BRIGHTON
General and antiques market every
Saturday in Upper Gardner St;
paintings market daily (May to
September) in King's Road
Local auctioneers: Hove Auction
Galleries, 115 Church Road, Hove
HAILSHAM
Market day Wednesdays
Local auctioneers: Burtenshaw
Walker, Market Square
HASTINGS
Market Monday to Saturday in
George Street; every Wednesday in
Cross Street, St Leonard's-on-Sea
Local auctioneers: Ascent Auction
Galleries, 11 East Ascent Street, St
Leonard's
HEATHFIELD
Market day Tuesdays
Local auctioneers: E. Watson &
Sons, 27 High Street
MAGHAM DOWN
Afternoon market the second

Wednesday of every month
RYE
General market in Rope Street every
Thursday; antiques market daily in
Strand Warehouses; antiques
market daily in summer and on
Wednesdays, Thursdays and
Saturdays in winter at the Old Daily
Market, Cinque Ports Street
Local auctioneers: Vidler & Co,
Cinque Ports Street
SEAFORD
Market day Saturdays
Local auctioneers: Newhaven
Auction Rooms

Essex

COLCHESTER
Market day Saturdays
Local auctioneers: Paskell & Cann,
11/14 East Hill; Reeman, Dansie
Howe & Son, Head Gate and 16
Crouch Street
MANNINGTREE
Market day Saturdays
Local auctioneers: Herbert Yeates &
Co, 17 South Street

Gloucester

BERKELEY
Market days Fridays and Saturdays
CHELTENHAM
Market day Thursdays
Local auctioneers: Lawson &
Lawson, 3 Regent Street
CIRENCESTER
Market day Fridays
Local auctioneers: R. A. Bennett &
Partners, 29 Sheep Street
DURSLEY
Market days Thursdays and Fridays
Local auctioneers: Davis, Champion
& Payne, 12/16 Long Street
GLOUCESTER
Market day Saturdays
Local auctioneers: Bruton Knowles
& Co, Cattle Market, St Oswalds
Road

STROUD
Market day Saturdays
Local auctioneers: E. J. Rowell &
Co, 8 Rowcroft
TETBURY
Market held alternate Wednesdays
Local auctioneers: J. Pearce
Pope & Sons, Long Street
TEWKESBURY
Market days Wednesdays and
Saturdays
Local auctioneers: Moore, Lear &
Son, 39 High Street

Greater Manchester
ALTRINCHAM
Market days Tuesdays and
Saturdays
Local auctioneers: David Morrison
& Son, Central Auction Galleries
ASHTON-UNDER-LYNE
Market open daily except Tuesdays
BOLTON
Ashburner Street market open
Tuesdays, Thursdays and
Saturdays; Knowsley Street market
open daily except Wednesday
afternoons and Sundays
Local auctioneers: Airey Entwistle,
30 Cross Street
BURY
Outdoor market on Wednesdays,
Fridays and Saturdays
Local auctioneers: Parkinson, Son &
Hamer, 14 Bolton Street
DENTON
Market days Fridays and Saturdays
FARNWORTH
Market days Mondays, Fridays and
Saturdays
HEYWOOD
Market days Fridays and Saturdays
HORWICH
Market days Tuesdays and
Saturdays
HYDE
Open market on Wednesdays,
Fridays and Saturdays
MANCHESTER
Church Street market open
Mondays to Saturdays; open market

at Civic Centre, Wythenshawe, held
on Tuesdays, Fridays and
Saturdays; open market at
Gortoncross Street, Gorton, on
Tuesdays, Fridays and Saturdays
Local auctioneers: Artingstall &
Hind, Deansgate, Knott Mill,
Manchester 3; Capes Dunn & Co, 38
Charles Street, Manchester 1; M.
Isaacs & Son, 10 Booth Street,
Manchester 3; Manchester Auction
Mart, 2/4 Atkinson Street, off
Deansgate, Manchester 3
MIDDLETON
Market day Fridays
OLDHAM
Specialist second-hand and antiques
market on Tommyfield open on
Wednesdays
Local auctioneers: Mills & Radcliffe,
101 Union Street
ROCHDALE
Market open daily except Tuesdays
STOCKPORT
Market days Tuesdays, Fridays and
Saturdays
URMSTON
Market days Tuesdays, Fridays and
Saturdays
WIGAN
Markets at Ashton (open Tuesdays
and Saturdays); Atherton (open
Fridays); Hindley (open Fridays);
Leigh (open Wednesdays, Fridays
and Saturdays); and Tyldesley (open
Fridays)
Local auctioneers: Healy Simpson &
Co, 11 King Street

Hampshire
ALDERSHOT
Market day Thursdays
Local auctioneers: Pearson's, 119
Victoria Road
BASINGSTOKE
Market days Wednesdays and
Saturdays
Local auctioneers: Pearson's, 27
London Street
EASTLEIGH
Market day Thursdays

Local auctioneers: Paul Rendle &
Co, 10 Romsey Road
FAREHAM
Market day Mondays
FARNBOROUGH
Market day Tuesdays
FLEET
Market day Saturdays
LYMINGTON
Market day Saturdays
Local auctioneers: Elliott & Green,
40 High Street
PORTSMOUTH
Market days Thursdays, Fridays and
Saturdays
Local auctioneers: D. M. Nesbit &
Co, 7 Clarendon Road
RINGWOOD
Market day Wednesdays
Local auctioneers: Ormiston's,
Cattle Market
SOUTHAMPTON
Market days Fridays and Saturdays
Local auctioneers: Southampton
Auction Rooms, 14a Paynes Road,
Shirley
WINCHESTER
Market days Wednesdays and
Fridays in Middle Brook Street;
Saturdays in British Rail car park
Local auctioneers: Chandler's, The
Broadway; Weller Eggar, Great
Minster Street

Hereford & Worcester

BROMSGROVE
Market days Tuesdays, Fridays and
Saturdays
Local auctioneers: A. Victor Powell,
12 St John's Street
DROITWICH
Market day Saturdays
EVESHAM
Market day Saturdays
Local auctioneers: Jackson-Stops &
Staff, High Street, Chipping
Campden; Arthur G. Griffiths &
Sons, 91 High Street, Evesham

HEREFORD
Market day Wednesdays
Local auctioneers: Duncan Heins &
Son, 24 Widemarsh Street; Linden
Alcock & Co, 8/9 Bridge Street
KIDDERMINSTER
Market days Thursdays and
Saturdays
Local auctioneers: Cattell & Young,
31 Worcester Street
KINGTON
Market day Thursdays
LEDBURY
Market day Tuesdays
LEOMINSTER
Market day Fridays
Local auctioneers: Russell Baldwin
& Bright, 38 South Street; Stooke,
Hill & Co, 3 Broad Street
PERSHORE
Market held Mondays to Fridays
inclusive
REDDITCH
Market days Tuesdays and
Saturdays
Local auctioneers: Bristows & Sutor,
135 Evesham Road
ROSS-ON-WYE
Market days Thursdays and
Saturdays
Local auctioneers: Coles Knapp &
Kennedy, Cattle Market
TENBURY WELLS
Market day Tuesdays
WORCESTER
Market day Saturdays
Local auctioneers: Thomas R. Jones
& Co, 6 Foregate Street; J. G. Lear
& Son, 46 Foregate Street

Hertfordshire

BISHOPS STORTFORD
Market days Thursdays and
Saturdays
Local auctioneers: Watson's 27
North Street; G. E. Sworder & Sons,
19 North Street
HATFIELD
Market days Wednesdays and
Saturdays

163

HEMEL HEMPSTEAD
Market days Thursdays, Fridays and Saturdays
Local auctioneers: Poulter & Francis, 57 Marlowes

HERTFORD
Market day Saturdays
Local auctioneers: Norris & Duvall, 106 Fore Street

HITCHIN
Market days Tuesdays and Saturdays
Local auctioneers: George Jackson & Son, Paynes Park

HODDESDON
Market day Wednesdays
Local auctioneers: W. H. Lee & Co, 70 High Street

ROYSTON
Market days Wednesdays and Saturdays
Local auctioneers: Douglas L. January, 2/3 Fish Hill

ST ALBANS
Market day Saturdays
Local auctioneers: Humberts, 6 Romeland

STEVENAGE
Market days Fridays and Saturdays
Local auctioneers: Richardson's, 86 High Street

TRING
Market day Fridays
Local auctioneers: Brown & Merry, Brook Street

WARE
Market day Tuesdays

WATFORD
Market days Tuesdays, Fridays and Saturdays

Humberside

BEVERLEY
Market days Tuesdays and Wednesdays

BRIDLINGTON
Market days Wednesdays and Saturdays
Local auctioneers: Broader & Spencer, The Imperial and Repository Salerooms, 18 Quay Road

BRIGG
Market days Tuesdays, Thursdays and Saturdays
Local auctioneers: Henry Spencer & Sons, 75 Wrawby Street; Dickinson, Davy & Markham, 10 Wrawby Street

DRIFFIELD
Market days Thursdays and Saturdays
Local auctioneers: Dee & Atkinson, The Exchange Saleroom

GOOLE
Market days Wednesdays, Fridays and Saturdays
Local auctioneers: Clegg & Son, 68 Aire Street

HULL
Market days Tuesdays, Fridays and Saturdays
Local auctioneers: R. R. Leonard & Son, 512 Holderness Road

SCUNTHORPE
Market held Mondays to Saturdays inclusive
Local auctioneers: Henry Spencer & Sons, 31 Oswald Road

WITHERNSEA
Market days Thursdays, Saturdays and Sundays

Kent

ASHFORD
General market every Saturday, with antiques stalls
Local auctioneers: Hobbs Parker, North Street; Burrows & Day, 39 Bank Street; Finn-Kelcey Ashenden Vidler & Co, Market Office and High Street

CANTERBURY
Market day Wednesdays
Local auctioneers: Worsfolds, 40 Station Road; Scarlett & Berthoud, 27 Watling Street

DARTFORD
Market day Thursdays
DEAL
Street market every Saturday
DOVER
Market day Saturdays
Local auctioneers: James B. Terson
& Son, 27/29 Castle Street
FAVERSHAM
Market days Wednesdays, Fridays
and Saturdays
FOLKESTONE
Antiques and produce in Old Town
Hall every Friday
Local auctioneers: Smith-Woolley &
Perry, Saleroom, 24 Dover Road
GRAVESEND
Market every day except Sundays
HERNE BAY
Market every Saturday plus Bank
Holidays
Local auctioneers: E. Iggulden &
Sons, 128 High Street
MAIDSTONE
General market with antiques every
Tuesday; furniture and bric-à-brac
every other Thursday; both at
Lockmeadow
Local auctioneers: B. Norris, The
Quest, Harrietsham; Walter &
Forknall, King Street
MARGATE
Market day Tuesdays from April to
September
Local auctioneers: Daniels (Kent)
Ltd, 81 High Street, Broadstairs
RAMSGATE
General market in Harbour every
day except Sundays
Local auctioneers: Leslie Hogbin &
Partners, 48 Queen Street
ROCHESTER
Market days Fridays and Saturdays
SANDWICH
Market day Thursdays
Local auctioneers: John Hogbin &
Son, Cattle Market
SEVENOAKS
General market at Cattle Market
every Wednesday
Local auctioneers: Parson's, Welch

& Cowell, 129 High Street
SHEERNESS
Market day Tuesdays
SITTINGBOURNE
Market day Fridays
Local auctioneers: G. W. Finn &
Sons, 3 Albany Road
SWANLEY
Market day Wednesdays
TENTERDEN
Market day Fridays
Local auctioneers: Butler & Hatch
Waterman (where I bought the
world-record-breaking Goss), High
Street; John Hogbin & Son, High
Street
WHITSTABLE
Market day Thursdays and Local
auctioneers: Harris & Co, 4 High
Street; J. T. Reeves & Son, Ltd, 15a
High Street

Lancashire

ACCRINGTON
Market days Tuesdays, Fridays and
Saturdays
Local auctioneers: Duckworth's 7 St
James Street
BACUP
Market days Wednesdays and
Saturdays
BARNOLDSWICK
Market day Saturdays
Local auctioneers: J. & J. Marshall,
7 St James Square
BLACKBURN
Market days Wednesdays, Fridays
and Saturdays
Local auctioneers: The Salerooms,
Lambeth Street
BLACKPOOL
Market open every day except
Sundays
Local auctioneers: E. Gordon
Round, 4 Bloomfield Road
BURNLEY
Open market Mondays, Thursdays
and Saturdays
Local auctioneers: Hammerton
Street Auction Rooms, 55

Hammerton Street
CHORLEY
Indoor market Tuesdays, Fridays and Saturdays. Open air market every Tuesday
Local auctioneers: Smith & Hodgkinson, 53 St Thomas's Road
CLITHEROE
Market days Tuesdays and Saturdays
Local auctioneers: Jas Barlow & Son, 16 Claremont Avenue
COLNE
Open air market every Wednesday
Local auctioneers: Colne Auction Sales, Queens Gur, Burnley Road
DARWEN
Market days Mondays, Fridays and Saturdays
Local auctioneers: Geoffrey Taylor & Co, 7 Market Street
FLEETWOOD
Market open Mondays, Tuesdays and Fridays in summer; Tuesdays and Fridays in winter
Local auctioneers: Harry Banks & Co, 52 Adelaide Street
HASLINGDEN
Small market open Tuesdays and Fridays
KIRKHAM
Market day Thursdays
LANCASTER
Market open every day except Sundays. Auction mart every Monday, Tuesday and Friday
Local auctioneers: T. Armitstead & Son, 26 King Street
MORECAMBE
Market open Mondays, Tuesdays and Fridays but closed Mondays in winter
Local auctioneers: Knight's National, 30 Victoria Street
NELSON
Open market every Wednesday, Friday and Saturday
Local auctioneers: M. & W. Pennine Salerooms, Colne Road, Brierfield
ORMSKIRK
Street market every Thursday and Saturday
PRESTON
Market days Mondays, Wednesdays, Fridays and Saturdays
Local auctioneers: Scantique, Hesketh Street; Let's Make A Deal, Adelphi Place
RAWTENSTALL
Market days Thursdays and Saturdays

Leicestershire

ASHBY-DE-LA-ZOUCH
Market day Saturdays
Local auctioneers: Stevenson & Barratt, 58 Market Street
COALVILLE
Market days Fridays and Saturdays
Local auctioneers: Garton's, 2 Belvoir Road
HINCKLEY
Market days Mondays and Saturdays
Local auctioneers: Hackney & Sons, 16a Station Road
LEICESTER
Open market held every day except Sundays
Local auctioneers: Oadby & Regency Auctions; Tarratt's, 16 Market Street; Arthur Collin, Loseby Lane
LOUGHBOROUGH
Market days Thursdays and Saturdays
Local auctioneers: Frank Innes, 3 Swan Street
LUTTERWORTH
Market day Thursdays
Local auctioneers: Howkins & Harrison, High Street
MARKET BOSWORTH
Market day Wednesdays
Local auctioneers: Hackney & Sons, Smithfield
MARKET HARBOROUGH
Market days Tuesdays and Saturdays
Local auctioneers: Market Harborough Auctions, Cattle Market

MELTON MOWBRAY
Market days Tuesdays and Saturdays
Local auctioneers: Startin's Auctions, 18 Park Road
OAKHAM
Market days Wednesdays and Saturdays
Local auctioneers: Norton's, The Saleroom, South Street
UPPINGHAM
Market day Fridays

Lincolnshire

ALFORD
Market days Tuesdays and Fridays
Local auctioneers: Mason's, 16 Market Place
BOSTON
Market days Wednesdays and Saturdays
Local auctioneers: Earl & Lawrence, 32 Wide Bargate; James Eley & Son, Boston Auction Rooms, Main Ridge
GRANTHAM
Market day Saturdays
Local auctioneers: Earl & Lawrence, 9 Watergate
HORNCASTLE
Market days Thursdays and Saturdays
Local auctioneers: Walter Woodroffe & Son, 3 South Street
LINCOLN
Central market days Fridays and Saturdays; Corn Market every Friday
Local auctioneers: Earl & Lawrence, 343 High Street; J. Hunter & Sons, 5 Newland
LOUTH
Market days Wednesdays, Fridays and Saturdays
Local auctioneers: Jackson, Green & Preston, Cattle Market; Dewer & Grant, Permanent House, Chequergate
MABLETHORPE
Market day Thursdays
Local auctioneers: Michael Emmitt

Organisation, 39 Victoria Road
MARKET RASEN
Market days Tuesdays and Wednesdays
Local auctioneers: Martin Maslin, 24 Market Place
SKEGNESS
Market held Fridays and Saturdays from October to April and daily in summer
Local auctioneers: Hardcastle & Son, 22 Drummond Road
SLEAFORD
Market days Mondays, Fridays and Saturdays
Local auctioneers: Earl & Lawrence, 55 Northgate
SPALDING
Market held daily, Tuesdays and Saturdays being best
Local auctioneers: Bob Gibson & Co, 2a High Street
SPILSBY
Market day Mondays
Local auctioneers: Simons & Co, 42 High Street
STAMFORD
Market days Fridays and Saturdays
Local auctioneers: Arthur E. Craig & Co, 14 St John's Street

London and Greater London

There are, of course, an enormous number of antiques auctioneers in the London area — far too many to list here. But the five leading fine art and chattels salerooms are:
Bonham's, Montpelier Galleries, Montpelier Street, London SW7. Regular sales of all manner of antiques
Christie's, 85 Old Brompton Road, London SW7. Regular sales of a wide range of antiques
Harrods Auction Galleries, Arundel Terrace, London SW13. Fortnightly sales throughout the year
Phillips, 7 Blenheim Street, London

W1. About ten sales every week covering all types of antiques and works of art

Sotheby's, 19 Motcomb Street, London SW1. Regular sales of antiques and fine art

London is famous for its street markets, most of which have antiques stalls. Some markets have gained reputations as good hunting grounds for the antiques buyer. The leading ones are:

Bayswater Antique Market, London W2: Open Monday to Saturday with the exception of Thursdays

Berwick Street, London W1: A bustling market in the heart of Soho. Open daily

Blackheath Antiques Market, London SE3: Held every Saturday

Camden Passage, London N1: Antiques of all shapes and sizes from a myriad of small shops and stalls. Open Mondays to Saturdays

Chapel Street Market, Islington, London N1: Held Thursdays, Fridays, Saturdays and Sunday mornings

Chelsea Antique Market, London SW3: Held in the King's Road, Monday to Saturday

Church Street, Edgware Road, London W2: Busy general market that also sells antiques. Open Mondays to Saturdays

The Cut Street Market, London SE1: Near Waterloo Station. Held Mondays to Saturdays

Earlham Street, London WC2: Mixed antiques and books from Monday to Saturday

Enfield, Middlesex: Thursdays and Saturdays in the old market square

Epping, Essex: Held Mondays along one side of the High Street

Epsom, Surrey: Saturdays only, close to the clock tower

Five Centuries Antique Fayre, Great Windmill Street, London W1: Eighteen stalls, open Monday to Friday

Greenwich Antiques Market, London SE10: Held every Saturday in Greenwich High Road

Hampstead, London NW3: Held Fridays and Saturdays just off the High Street

London Silver Vaults, Chancery Lane, London WC2: Underground market specialising in silverware, antique and modern. Open Mondays to Saturdays

Lyndhurst Hall Comic Market, Warden Road, London NW5: Yes, it really does specialise in comics and is open the first Friday of each month

Marylebone Antique Market, Crawford Street, London W1: Bric-à-brac and nice junk on sale Mondays to Saturdays

New Caledonian, Tower Bridge Road, London SE1: Enormous variety of collectables of every description. Fridays only

Portobello Road, London W11: Large number of antiques on sale. Open Monday to Saturday, with half day on Thursdays

South London Antiques Centre, Camberwell Road, London SE5: Open Tuesdays to Saturdays and from 2 to 6pm Sundays for the trade only

Up The Market, Shorts Gardens, London WC2: Antiques sold Mondays to Saturdays

Merseyside

BIRKENHEAD
Permanent market open every day except Sundays
Local auctioneers: Baker, Baker & Richard, Hamilton Street
GARSTON
Market Tuesdays and Saturdays
LIVERPOOL
Main markets at St John's Centre (open six days a week) and St Martin's Market, Great Homer Street (open daily except Wednesday)

Local auctioneers: Marsh Lyons & Co, 19 Dale Street; Outhwaite & Litherland, Fontenoy Street

SOUTHPORT
Market open every day except Tuesday afternoons
Local auctioneers: Ellis & Sons, 459 Lord Street

Norfolk

ACLE
Market day Thursdays
ANMER
Market day Saturdays
ATTLEBOROUGH
Market day Thursdays
AYLSHAM
Market day Mondays
Local auctioneers: William A. Frazer, 32 Red Lion Street; G. A. Key, 8 Market Place
BURNHAM MARKET
Market day Mondays
DISS
Market day Fridays
Local auctioneers: Thos Gaze & Son, Roydon Road
DOWNHAM MARKET
Market day Fridays
Local auctioneers: C. Hawkins & Sons, Lynn Road
EAST DEREHAM
Market day Fridays
Local auctioneers: Case & Dewing, Church Street, Dereham
EAST HARLING
Market day Tuesdays
Local auctioneers: J. Johnson, Allen & Sons, Market Street
FAKENHAM
Market day Thursdays
Local auctioneers: C. C. H. Beck, The Oaks, Oak Street
HARLESTON
Market day Wednesdays
Local auctioneers: G. Durrant & Son, 34 Thoroughfare
HOLT
Market day Fridays

KING'S LYNN
Market days Tuesdays and Saturdays
Local auctioneers: Bonhams, Middleton Tower; C. Hawkins & Sons, Bank Chambers
NORTH WALSHAM
Market day Thursdays
Local auctioneers: G. A. Key, 43 Market Place
NORWICH
Market days Mondays to Saturdays
Local auctioneers: G. A. Key, 8 Market Place, Aylsham
STALHAM
Market day Tuesdays
Local auctioneers: Brian E. Boning, Brant House, Wayford
SWAFFHAM
Market day Saturdays
Local auctioneers: C. Hawkins & Sons, 19a Market Place
THETFORD
Market day Saturdays
Local auctioneers: Rutters, 47 King Street
WATTON
Market day Thursdays
Local auctioneers: Noel D. Abel, 32 Norwich Road
WELLS-NEXT-THE-SEA
Market day Wednesdays
YARMOUTH
Market days Wednesdays and Saturdays
Local auctioneers: Aldreds, 17 Hall Quay; John Howard & Partners, 33 Regent Street

Northamptonshire

CORBY
Market days Fridays and Saturdays
Local auctioneers: Wilson & Partners, 16 Queen Street
DAVENTRY
Market days Tuesdays and Saturdays
Local auctioneers: Merry Sons & Cowling, 48 High Street

KETTERING
Market days Fridays and Saturdays
Local auctioneers: Berry Bros &
Legge, Market Place
NORTHAMPTON
Market days Wednesdays, Fridays
and Saturdays
Local auctioneers: Berry Bros &
Legge, 14 Castilian Street
OUNDLE
Market day Thursdays
PETERBOROUGH
Market days Wednesdays, Fridays
and Saturdays
Local auctioneers: Lyall & Co, 1
Queen Street; Arthur E. Craig & Co,
Broadway Buildings
THRAPSTON
Market days Tuesdays and
Thursdays
Local auctioneers: Henry Bletsoe &
Son, High Street
WELLINGBOROUGH
Market days Wednesdays and
Saturdays
Local auctioneers: Berry Bros &
Legge, 8 Sheep Street

Northumberland

ALNWICK
Market day Saturdays
Local auctioneers: Harry Humble,
East Cawledge Park Farm
BERWICK-UPON-TWEED
Market days Wednesdays and
Saturdays
Local auctioneers: Auction
Galleries, Mount Road,
Tweedmouth
HEXHAM
Market day Tuesdays
Local auctioneers: Coleman's of
Hexham, 15 St Mary's Chase
MORPETH
Market day Wednesdays
Local auctioneers: Addison Hudson,
22 Newgate Street

Nottinghamshire

HUCKNALL
Market day Fridays
MANSFIELD
Market held every day
Local auctioneers: Graham's
Auctions (Mansfield) Ltd, Cattle
Market
NEWARK
Market days Wednesdays and
Saturdays
Local auctioneers: Earl & Lawrence,
24 Cartergate
NEW OLLERTON
Market day Wednesdays
NOTTINGHAM
Central market daily; Sneinton
market held Mondays and Saturdays
Local auctioneers: Walker Walton
Hanson (Auctions), The Nottingham
Auction Mart, Byard Lane
RETFORD
Market days Thursdays and
Saturdays
Local auctioneers: Henry Spencer &
Sons, 20 The Square
SOUTHWELL
Market day Saturdays
Local auctioneers: Theobalds,
Beardsley, 14 Westgate
SUTTON-IN-ASHFIELD
Market days Fridays and Saturdays
WARSOP
Market days Fridays and Saturdays
Local auctioneers: Peter H. Milner,
26a High Street
WORKSOP
Market days Wednesdays, Fridays
and Saturdays
Local auctioneers: Henry Spencer &
Sons, 91 Bridge Street

Oxfordshire

BANBURY
Market days Thursdays and
Saturdays
Local auctioneers: Buckell &
Ballard, 49 Parsons Street

BICESTER
Market days Mondays and Fridays
Local auctioneers: E. P. Messenger
& Son, 27 Sheep Street
CHIPPING NORTON
Market day Wednesdays
Local auctioneers: Buckell &
Ballard, 12 New Street
DIDCOT
Market day Fridays
Local auctioneers: Adkins & Co, 8
Bartholomew Street
FARINGDON
Market day Tuesdays
Local auctioneers: Hobbs &
Chambers, 16 Market Place
HENLEY-ON-THAMES
Market days Mondays, Wednesdays
and Saturdays
Local auctioneers: J. Chambers &
Co, 17 Hart Street
KIDLINGTON
Market day Tuesdays
Local auctioneers: Buckell &
Ballard, 18 High Street
OXFORD
Market day Wednesdays
Local auctioneers: Phillips, 39 Park
End Street; Lord & Chapman, 38
South Parade
THAME
Market day Tuesdays
WANTAGE
Market days Wednesdays and
Saturdays
Local auctioneers: Buckell &
Ballard, 1/2 Market Place

Shropshire

BRIDGNORTH
Market day Saturdays
Local auctioneers: Perry & Phillips,
Listley Street
CHURCH STRETTON
Market day Thursdays
ELLESMERE
Market day Tuesdays
LUDLOW
Market days Fridays and Saturdays
Local auctioneers: McCartney

Morris & Barker, Portcullis Hall
MARKET DRAYTON
Market day Wednesdays
Local auctioneers: Barber & Son, 2
Cheshire Street
NEWPORT
Market days Fridays and Saturdays
OSWESTRY
Market day Wednesdays
SHREWSBURY
Market days Wednesdays, Fridays
and Saturdays
Local auctioneers: Hall, Wateridge
& Owen, Welsh Bridge
WELLINGTON
Market days Tuesdays, Thursdays
and Saturdays
WHITCHURCH
Market day Fridays

Somerset

BRIDGWATER
Market day Wednesdays
Local auctioneers: W. R. J.
Greenslade & Co, 33 High Street
CHARD
Market day Saturdays
CHEDDAR
Market day Wednesdays
FROME
Market days Wednesdays and
Saturdays
Local auctioneers: Abbott Castle, 7
Badcox
GLASTONBURY
Market day Tuesdays
Local auctioneers: Cooper &
Tanner, George Street
ILMINSTER
Market day every other Wednesday
SHEPTON MALLETT
Market day Fridays
Local auctioneers: Cooper &
Tanner, 44a Commercial Road
TAUNTON
Market days Tuesdays and
Saturdays
Local auctioneers: W. R. J.
Greenslade & Co, 2 and 13 Hammet
Street

171

WELLS
Market days Wednesdays and Saturdays
Local auctioneers: Cluttons, 10 New Street

YEOVIL
Market days Mondays and Fridays
Local auctioneers: R. B. Taylor & Sons, Princes Street

Staffordshire

BRERETON
Market days Tuesdays, Thursdays and Saturdays

BURTON-ON-TRENT
Market days Thursdays and Saturdays
Local auctioneers: Arnold & Son, 13 Market Place

CANNOCK
Market days Tuesdays, Fridays and Saturdays

LEEK
Market day Saturdays
Local auctioneers: Charles Butters & Sons, 38 Derby Road

LICHFIELD
Market day Mondays

RUGELEY
Market days Tuesdays, Thursdays and Saturdays
Local auctioneers: Wintertons, 18 Brook Square

STAFFORD
Market days Tuesdays, Fridays and Saturdays
Local auctioneers: Evans & Evans, Greengate Street

STOKE
Market days Wednesdays, Fridays and Saturdays
Local auctioneers: Louis Taylor & Sons, Percy Street, Hanley

STONE
Market day Thursdays
Local auctioneers: Robert S. Heywood, Lichfield Road

UTTOXETER
Market day Saturdays
Local auctioneers: Bagshaws, 17 High Street

Suffolk

BECCLES
Market day Fridays
Local auctioneers: Savills, 23 New Market Place

BRANDON
Market day Thursdays

BUNGAY
Market day Thursdays

BURY ST EDMUNDS
Market days Wednesdays and Saturdays
Local auctioneers: Lacy Scott & Sons, 3 Hatter Street

HALESWORTH
Market day alternate Wednesdays
Local auctioneers: Hanbury Williams, 26 Market Place

HAVERHILL
Market day Fridays

IPSWICH
Market days Tuesdays and Saturdays
Local auctioneers: E. R. Webster & Son, Great Colman Street Chambers

LOWESTOFT
Market days Wednesdays and Saturdays
Local auctioneers: Notleys, 2 Imperial House, Bevan Street

MILDENHALL
Market day Fridays

NEWMARKET
Market days Tuesdays and Saturdays
Local auctioneers: Douglas January & Partners, 124 High Street

SAXMUNDHAM
Market day alternate Wednesdays

STOWMARKET
Market day Thursdays. Covered market Saturdays
Local auctioneers: B. C. Knight & Sons, Market Place; Paul Wright & Co, Ltd, 21 Ipswich Street; Abbotts, 42 Ipswich Street

SUDBURY
Market day Thursdays
Local auctioneers: Jennings &
Sworders, 87 North Street
WICKHAM MARKET
Market day Mondays
Local auctioneers: James Abbott,
The Hill; A. E. Spencer & Sons, The
Hill
WOODBRIDGE
Market day Thursdays
Local auctioneers: Dennis Neal, 28
Church Street

Surrey

CHERTSEY
Market day Saturdays
CRANLEIGH
Market day Thursdays
DORKING
Market day Fridays
Local auctioneers: Regent Auction
Galleries, 141/143 High Street
EPSOM
Market day Saturdays
Local auctioneers: Edwards &
Sharp, 112 High Street
GODALMING
Market day Fridays
Local auctioneers: Messenger, May
& Baverstock, Auction Rooms, 93
High Street
GUILDFORD
General market every Wednesday
Local auctioneers: Cubitt & West, 44
High Street; Clarke Gammon,
Bedford Road
HORLEY
Market day Saturdays
REDHILL
Market day Thursdays
Local auctioneers: Harold Williams
Bennett & Partners, 2/3 South
Parade, Merstham
WOKING
Market days Tuesdays, Fridays and
Saturdays
Local auctioneers: Chancellor's &
Co, 38 Commercial Way; Barber's
77 Chertsey Road

Tyne and Wear

SOUTH SHIELDS
Market days Mondays and
Saturdays
Local auctioneers: Anderson &
Garland, Market Street, Newcastle;
I. Goldman, 70 Ocean Road
WHITLEY BAY
Market days Tuesdays, Thursdays
and Saturdays
Local auctioneers: Featonby's
234/236 Park View

Warwickshire

ATHERSTONE
Market days Tuesdays and Fridays
HENLEY-IN-ARDEN
Market days Mondays, Wednesdays
and Saturdays
Local auctioneers: Henley-in-Arden
Auction Sales Ltd, Cattle Market,
Warwick Road
RUGBY
Market day Mondays
Local auctioneers: Howkins &
Harrison, 12 Albert Street
SHIPSTON-ON-STOUR
Market day Wednesdays
STRATFORD-UPON-AVON
Market day Fridays
Local auctioneers: Howkins &
Harrison, 24 Sheep Street
WARWICK
Market day Saturdays
Local auctioneers: Bright, Willis, 3
Jury Street

West Midlands

BIRMINGHAM
Market held Mondays to Fridays
inclusive
COVENTRY
Market days Wednesdays, Fridays
and Saturdays
Local auctioneers: Ward & Halbert,
112 Walsgrave Road
DUDLEY
Market days Mondays to Saturdays

Local auctioneers: Cecil Cariss & Son, Priory Street

HALESOWEN
Market days Tuesdays, Fridays and Saturdays
Local auctioneers: Raymond Morgan & Co, 20a Hagley Street

NUNEATON
Market day Saturdays

OLDBURY
Market days Tuesdays and Saturdays

ROWLEY REGIS
Market days Mondays and Saturdays

SMETHWICK
Market days Fridays and Saturdays
Local auctioneers: Jones Son & Vernon, 39 Waterloo Road

STOURBRIDGE
Market held Mondays to Saturdays inclusive
Local auctioneers: Smithfield Saleroom, Smithfield

WALSALL
Market days Tuesdays and Saturdays

WEDNESBURY
Market days Fridays and Saturdays
Local auctioneers: Wednesbury Auctions, Rydding Lane, West Bromwich

WEST BROMWICH
Market days Mondays, Fridays and Saturdays
Local auctioneers: Wednesbury Auctions, Rydding Lane

WOLVERHAMPTON
Market days Wednesdays, Fridays and Saturdays
Local auctioneers: Pitchers Saleroom, 47 Lichfield Street

West Sussex

ARUNDEL
Daily antiques and collectors' market, including Sundays in summer
Local auctioneers: Phillip Barrett, 49 High Street

BURGESS HILL
Market days Wednesdays and Saturdays

CHICHESTER
Market held every day except Sundays
Local auctioneers: Stride & Son, Southdown House, St John's Street

CRAWLEY
Street market held every Tuesday, Thursday, Friday and Saturday

EAST GRINSTEAD
Street market every Saturday

HAYWARDS HEATH
Market day Sundays
Local auctioneers: Sussex Auction Galleries, 59 Perrymount Road

LEWES
Market day Tuesdays
Local auctioneers: Gorringe's 15 North Street

LITTLEHAMPTON
Market days Fridays and Saturdays
Local auctioneers: Hexton & Cheney, 3 Pier Road

WORTHING
Market day Saturdays
Local auctioneers: Fox & Sons, Rivoli Auction Galleries, Chapel Road

Wiltshire

CALNE
Market day Fridays

CHIPPENHAM
Market day Fridays
Local auctioneers: Clifford Drewett & Co, 34 Market Place

DEVIZES
Market days Thursdays and Saturdays
Local auctioneers: Devizes Market Auctioneers, 15 Market Place

MARLBOROUGH
Market days Wednesdays and Saturdays
Local auctioneers: A. W. Neate & Sons, 93 High Street; David Garside, 30 High Street

SALISBURY
Market days Tuesdays and Saturdays
Local auctioneers: Humberts, 8 Rotherstone Road

SWINDON
Market day Mondays
Local auctioneers: Fielder, Jones & Gale, 8 High Street; Cox & Billingham, 57 Commercial Road

TROWBRIDGE
Market days Tuesdays, Fridays and Saturdays
Local auctioneers: Abbott Castle, 3 Roundstone Street

WARMINSTER
Market day Fridays
Local auctioneers: John Cotton, 36 East Street

WESTBURY
Market day Tuesdays

Yorkshire

BARNSLEY
Market days Wednesdays and Saturdays
Local auctioneers: Beech Street Sales, 20 Beech Street

BATLEY
Market days Fridays and Saturdays

BAWTRY
Market held every day from Mondays to Saturdays

BEDALE
Market days Tuesdays and Thursdays
Local auctioneers: Dales Furniture Hall, The Bridge; Bedale Auction Mart, Bridge Street

BINGLEY
Market days Wednesdays and Fridays
Local auctioneers: Bingley Auction Mart, Keighley Road

BOROUGHBRIDGE
Market days Mondays and Tuesdays
Local auctioneers: Boroughbridge Auction Mart, Market Hall

BRADFORD
Market held every day from Mondays to Saturdays, excluding Wednesdays
Local auctioneers: Henry Spencer & Sons, 4 Up Piccadilly

BRIGHOUSE
Market days Wednesdays and Saturdays
Local auctioneers: C. J. Dyson, 37 Bethel Street; Mawson & Walton, 116 Commercial Street

DEWSBURY
Market days Wednesdays and Saturdays
Local auctioneers: Dewsbury Auctions, 629 Huddersfield Road

DONCASTER
Market days Tuesdays, Fridays and Saturdays
Local auctioneers: Stanilands, 28 Netherall Road

EASINGWOLD
Market days Tuesdays and Fridays
Local auctioneers: G. Summersgill, Spring Street

ELLAND
Market day Fridays
Local auctioneers: Walker, Singleton & Co, Auction Centre, Saddleworth Road, West Vale

GOLDTHORPE
Market day Saturdays

HELMSLEY
Market day Fridays

HOLMFIRTH
Market day Thursdays
Local auctioneers: Wm Sykes & Sons, 38 Huddersfield Road

HUDDERSFIELD
Market day Mondays
Local auctioneers: Armitage, Hewitt & Hellowell, 32 Queen Street

INGLETON
Market day Fridays

KEIGHLEY
Market days Wednesdays, Fridays and Saturdays
Local auctioneers: Ackroyd & Sons, 126 Skipton Road

KIRKBYMOORSIDE
Market day Wednesdays
KNARESBOROUGH
Market days Mondays and Wednesdays
LEEDS
Market days Tuesdays, Fridays and Saturdays
Local auctioneers: G. Parkin & Co, Canal Wharf, Water Lane, Leeds 11
LEYBURN
Market day Fridays
MALTBY
Market day Fridays
MALTON
Market days Fridays and Saturdays
Local auctioneers: Boulton & Cooper Ltd, The Milton Rooms
MASHAM
Market day Wednesdays
MORLEY
Market held Tuesdays to Saturdays inclusive
Local auctioneers: Central Auction Mart, Britannia Road
NORTHALLERTON
Market days Wednesdays and Saturdays
Local auctioneers: Northallerton Auctions Ltd, Applegarth
OSSETT
Market days Tuesdays and Fridays
Local auctioneers: Chas. W. Harrison & Son, Ashfield House, Illingworth Street
PICKERING
Market day Mondays
Local auctioneers: Boulton & Cooper Ltd, St Georges House, Market Place
PONTEFRACT
Market day Saturdays
Local auctioneers: Harrisons, 10 Ropergate
PUDSEY
Market days Tuesdays, Fridays and Saturdays
Local auctioneers: Harry Ward & Sons, 7 Town Street, Stanningley
RICHMOND
Market day Saturdays

Local auctioneers: Norman F. Brown, Rosemary House
RIPON
Market day Thursdays
Local auctioneers: Renton & Renton, 12 Queen Street
ROTHERHAM
Market days Mondays and Saturdays
Local auctioneers: Henry Spencer & Sons, 12 The Crofts, Moorgate
SCARBOROUGH
Market day Thursdays
Local auctioneers: H. C. Chapman & Son, The Auction Mart, North Street; Boulton & Cooper Ltd, Crossgates
SELBY
Market day Mondays
Local auctioneers: Bartle & Son, James Street
SETTLE
Market day Tuesdays
Local auctioneers: James Thompson, Church Street
SHEFFIELD
Market held Mondays to Saturdays inclusive except Thursdays
Local auctioneers: Goff Auction Galleries, Wellington Street
SHIPLEY
Market day Fridays
SKIPTON
Market held Mondays, Wednesdays, Fridays and Saturdays
Local auctioneers: Hepper Watson & Sons, 6 Sheep Street
STOKESLEY
Market day Fridays
Local auctioneers: Appleton, Ralph & Hall, 26 College Square
THIRSK
Market days Mondays and Saturdays
Local auctioneers: James H. Burns, 19 Market Place
THORNE
Market days Fridays and Saturdays
TODMORDEN
Market days Wednesdays, Fridays and Saturdays

WAKEFIELD
Market days Mondays, Fridays and Saturdays
Local auctioneers: Chas. W. Harrison, Crown Court, Wood Street
WETHERBY
Market day Thursdays
Local auctioneers: H. D. Hill, Shaw's Barn Lane, Linton Road
WHITBY
Market days Mondays and Wednesdays

Local auctioneers: Clarence Salerooms, Baxtergate
WOMBWELL
Market days Fridays and Saturdays
YORK
Market held Tuesdays to Saturdays inclusive
Local auctioneers: Christie's 46 Bootham, York 3; Ernest Crampton & Sons Ltd, Bar Auction Rooms, Toft Garden

SCOTLAND

Former county names are listed
under regional headings as they are still widely used

Borders Region
Peeblesshire

PEEBLES
Market day Fridays
Local auctioneers: Lawrie &
Symington, Yardman's House

Central Region
Stirlingshire

FALKIRK
Market day Tuesdays
Local auctioneers: Falkirk Auction,
208 Grahams Road
STIRLING
Market day Thursdays
Local auctioneers: J. Stewart, 14
Dumbarton Road

Dumfries and Galloway Region
Dumfriesshire

ANNAN
Market day Thursdays
DUMFRIES
Market day Wednesdays
Local auctioneers: Smiths Gore, 43
Castle Street
LOCKERBIE
Market day Thursdays
Local auctioneers: Harrison &
Hetherington Ltd
THORNHILL
Market day Thursdays
Local auctioneers: Nithsdale
Auction Mart

Kirkcudbrightshire

CASTLE DOUGLAS
Market days Mondays, Tuesdays
and Thursdays
Local auctioneers: Wallets Marts Ltd,
Auction Mart

Wigtownshire

NEWTON STEWART
Market day Wednesdays
Local auctioneers: James Craig Ltd,
Auction Mart
STRANRAER
Market day Fridays
Local auctioneers: James Craig Ltd,
Auction Mart

Fife Region
Fife

LETHAM
Market days Mondays and Fridays

Grampian Region
Aberdeenshire

ABERDEEN
Market day Fridays
Local auctioneers: Leslie Auctions
Ltd, 90 North Deeside Road, Culter;
John Mile, 9 North Silver Street
ABOYNE
Market day Mondays
ALFORD
Market day Fridays
ELLON
Market day Mondays
FRASERBURGH
Market day Wednesdays
HUNTLY
Market day Wednesdays
INVERURIE
Market day Thursdays
Local auctioneers: W. J. Lippe, 16
Selbie Drive

Banffshire

KEITH
Market day Tuesdays
Local auctioneers: Robert Hendry & Son

Kincardineshire

LAURENCEKIRK
Market days Mondays and alternate Saturdays
Local auctioneers: Kincardineshire Auction Mart, Mart Office

Highland Region

Caithness

THURSO
Market day Tuesdays
Local auctioneers: Hamilton's Auction Marts, Sale Yard
WICK
Market day Thursdays
Local auctioneers: Jas Sutherland, 19 and 23 Dempster Street

Inverness-shire

INVERNESS
Market days Tuesdays and Fridays
Local auctioneers: Hamilton's Auction Marts, Sale Yard

Nairnshire

NAIRN
Market day Thursdays

Ross and Cromarty

DINGWALL
Market day Wednesdays
Local auctioneers: Hamilton's Auction Marts, Sale Yard

Lothian Region

East Lothian

BATHGATE
Market day Mondays
HADDINGTON
Market day Fridays

Local auctioneers: Leslie & Leslie, Market Street

Midlothian

EDINBURGH
Market day Tuesdays
Local auctioneers: Phillips in Scotland, 65 George Street

Strathclyde Region

Argyllshire

OBAN
Market day Tuesdays
Local auctioneers: Thos Corson & Co, Auction Mart

Ayrshire

AYR
Market day Tuesdays
Local auctioneers: James Craig Ltd, Foreman's House
KILMARNOCK
Market day Fridays
Local auctioneers: R. B. Thomson, 16a West Langlands Street

Lanarkshire

LANARK
Market day Mondays
MOTHERWELL
Market day Tuesdays
WISHAW
Market day Fridays

Renfrewshire

ELDERSLIE
Market day Mondays
PAISLEY
Market day Mondays
Local auctioneers: Robt Paterson & Son, 8 Orchard Street

Tayside Region

Angus

DUNDEE
Market day Tuesdays

Local auctioneers: Robert McTear &
Co, 7 Ward Road; B. L. Fenton &
Sons, 84 Victoria Road
FORFAR
Market days Mondays and Fridays
Local auctioneers: Angus Marts Ltd,
12 Market Street

Kinross-shire
MILNATHORT
Market day Mondays

Perthshire
CRIEFF
Market day Tuesdays
Local auctioneers: William Neil &
Son, 22 Galvelmore Street
PERTH
Market days Mondays and Fridays
Local auctioneers: Thomas Love &
Sons Ltd, 12 St John's Place;
Bonham's, 8 Atholl Crescent

WALES

Clwyd

ABERGELE
Market day Mondays
Local auctioneers: R. Pearce & Co
Ltd, 61 Market Street
CORWEN
Market day Tuesdays
Local auctioneers: R. G. Jones Ltd,
Smithfield Buildings, The Terrace
DENBIGH
Market day Wednesdays
Local auctioneers: K. Hugh Dodd &
Partners, 25 Vale Street
FLINT
Market day Fridays
LLANGOLLEN
Market day Tuesdays
Local auctioneers: David Owen &
Co, 36 Castle Street
MOLD
Market day Wednesdays
Local auctioneers: K. Hugh Dodd &
Partners, Auction Galleries, Chester
Street
WREXHAM
Market days Mondays, Thursdays
and Saturdays
Local auctioneers: Jones & Son,
Salerooms, 48 Chester Street;
Wingett & Son, Chattel Auction
Room, 24/25 Chester Street

Dyfed

ABERYSTWYTH
Market day Mondays
Local auctioneers: Thomas Jones &
Son, 5 Terrace Road
CARDIGAN
Market day Saturdays
Local auctioneers: J. J. Morris, Priory
Street
CARMARTHEN
Market days Wednesdays and
Saturdays
Local auctioneers: Thomas Jones &
Son, Queen Street
CRYMMYCH
Market day Saturdays
FISHGUARD
Market day Thursdays
Local auctioneers: J. J. Morris, 16
Main Street
HAVERFORDWEST
Market days Tuesdays and
Saturdays
Local auctioneers: Basil Jones &
Sons, 14 Old Bridge
KILGETTY
Market day alternate Mondays
LAMPETER
Market held every other Tuesday
Local auctioneers: D. A. G. Jones, 2
Bridge Street, Aberaeron
LLANDEILO
Market day Saturdays
Local auctioneers: Walter James &
Son, Wedgwood Place
LLANDOVERY
Market held every Friday and
alternate Tuesdays
Local auctioneers: R. G. Daniel &
Partners, Mart Office
LLANELLI
Market days Thursdays and
Saturdays
Local auctioneers: Thomas Jones &
Son, 16 Murry Street
MILFORD HAVEN
Market day Fridays
Local auctioneers: Rees, Richards &
Partners, 16 Charles Street
NARBERTH
Market day alternate Thursdays
Local auctioneers: Richard Sykes,
Hill House, High Street; Bowling
Bros, Central Auction Rooms
NEWCASTLE EMLYN
Market day Fridays
Local auctioneers: Thomas Jones &
Son, Emlyn Square
PEMBROKE
Market day Fridays
Local auctioneers: John R. Bennion,

East Gate House
TREGARON
Market day alternate Tuesdays
WHITLAND
Market day Tuesdays

Gwent

ABERGAVENNY
Market days Tuesdays and Fridays
Local auctioneers: Montague Harris
& Co, 30 Lion Street; Russell
Baldwin & Bright; 47 Cross Street
ABERTILLERY
Market day Saturdays
BLACKWOOD
Market day Fridays
Local auctioneers: Seth Phillips &
Son, 105 High Street
MONMOUTH
Market days Fridays and alternate
Mondays
Local auctioneers: Coles Knapp &
Kennedy, 2 Agincourt Square
PONTYPOOL
Market days Wednesdays, Fridays
and Saturdays
Local auctioneers: Robt M. Cormack
& Sons, 28 George Street
USK
Market days Thursdays and
alternate Mondays
Local auctioneers: Digby Turner &
Co, 21 Bridge Street

Gwynedd

BANGOR
Small daily market
Local auctioneers: Jones & Davies,
Wellfield Chambers
CAERNARFON
Market day Saturdays
Local auctioneers: Chas Medforth &
Co, 38 Bridge Street
CONWY
Market held every Saturday and
Tuesday throughout summer
Local auctioneers: Griffith Morris
& Co, 5b High Street

DOLGELLAU
Market day Fridays
FAIRBOURNE
Market day Fridays
HOLYHEAD
Market day Saturdays
LLANGEFNI
Market day Thursdays
Local auctioneers: Morgan Evans &
Co, 27 Church Street
LLANRWST
Market day Tuesdays
Local auctioneers: Bob Parry & Co
Ltd, Smithfield
MENAI BRIDGE
Market day Mondays (mainly
fatstock)
PWLLHELI
Market day Wednesdays
Local auctioneers: Robert Parry &
Sons, 91 High Street

Mid Glamorgan

BRIDGEND
Market day Tuesdays
Local auctioneers: David Payton, 10
Dunraven Place
MAESTEG
Market day Fridays
NELSON
Market days Mondays and
Saturdays
NEWTON
Market day Tuesdays
Local auctioneers: Norman A. Lloyd
& Co, 16 Broad Street
PONTYPRIDD
Market days Wednesdays and
Saturdays
Local auctioneers: Pontypridd
Salerooms & Auction Mart, Lesser
Town Hall

Powys

BRECON
Market days Tuesdays and Fridays
BUILTH WELLS
Market day Mondays
Local auctioneers: Jones Bros, 40

High Street
CRICKHOWELL
Market day Thursdays
HAY-ON-WYE
Market days Mondays and
Thursdays
Local auctioneers: Russell Baldwin
& Bright, 5 Church Street
KNIGHTON
Market days Thursdays and Fridays
LLANFYLLIN
Market day Thursdays
Local auctioneers: Hubert Watkins,
Gwyndy
LLANIDLOES
Market day Saturdays
Local auctioneers: Morris, Marshall
& Poole, Great Oak Street
LLANWRTYD WELLS
Market day Thursdays
MACHYNLLETH
Market day Wednesdays
Local auctioneers: R. G. Jones Ltd,
Doll Street
PRESTEIGNE
Market day Wednesdays
RHAYADER
Market day Wednesdays
Local auctioneers: Campbell &
Edwards, 4 North Street

SENNYBRIDGE
Market held every Wednesday and
the second Friday of every month
WELSHPOOL
Market day Mondays
Local auctioneers: Williams &
Sambrook, 8 Church Street
YSTRADGYNLAIS
Market day Mondays

South Glamorgan

COWBRIDGE
Market day Mondays
Local auctioneers: Herbert R.
Thomas & Son, 59 High Street
WHITCHURCH
Market day Fridays

West Glamorgan

NEATH
Market held daily
Local auctioneers: Thomas,
Edwards & Anthony Morris, 33
Alfred Street
SWANSEA
Market days Wednesdays and
Saturdays
Local auctioneers: Stewart, Davies
& Evans, 62 Mansel Street

N. IRELAND

Antrim

BALLYMENA
Market day Saturdays
Local auctioneers:F. J. McCartney &
Crawford, 28 Thomas Street; J. H.
McKinney & Sons, Broadway
Avenue

BELFAST
Market days Tuesdays and Fridays
Local auctioneers: Alex Murdoch &
Deane, 11 Chichester Street, Belfast
1; John Ross & Co, 37 Montgomery
Street, Belfast 1; Kennedy &
Wolfenden Co Ltd, 161/163 Victoria
Street; Spences Auction Mart,
Bradbury Place, Belfast BT2 7AF

CARRICKFERGUS
Market day Thursdays

LARNE
Market day Wednesdays
Local auctioneers: D. J. McKenna, 11
Victoria Road

LISBURN
Market day Tuesdays
Local auctioneers: Sidney
Mawhinney, 18 Castle Street

RANDALSTOWN
Market day Wednesdays

TOOMEBRIDGE
Market day Tuesdays

Armagh

ARMAGH
Market day Tuesdays
Local auctioneers: T. Brooks & Co, 5
Dobbing Street

CROSSMAGLEN
Market day first Friday in every
month
Local auctioneers: Eugene
Hanratty, 7 Newry Street

KILLYLEA
Market held last Friday in the month

LURGAN
Market day Thursdays
Local auctioneers: Robert

Thompson & Son, 12 William Street

PORTADOWN
Market day Saturdays
Local auctioneers: Archie Gibson &
Son, 1 High Street

Down

BALLYNAHINCH
Market day Thursdays

BANGOR
Market day Wednesdays
Local auctioneers: Jas T. Brice &
Son, 139 Main Street

CASTLEWELLAN
Market day Mondays
Local auctioneers: James Wilson &
Son, 79 Main Street

COMBER
Market day Tuesdays
Local auctioneers: Thos Orr Ltd, 58
Castle Street

HILLTOWN
Market held second Tuesday in the
month

KILKEEL
Market day Wednesdays
Local auctioneers: Francis O'Hagan,
6 Greencastle Street

NEWRY
Market days Thursdays and
Saturdays
Local auctioneers: W. V. Hogg &
Son Ltd, 34 Merchants Quay; W.
Holt Garnett & Co Ltd, Cecil Street

RATHFRILAND
Market day Wednesdays

Fermanagh

IRVINESTOWN
Market day Wednesdays
Local auctioneers: John J. McElroy

LISNASKEA
Market day Saturdays

NEWTOWN BUTLER
Market held first Tuesday in the
month

Londonderry

DRAPERSTOWN
Market day Fridays
Local auctioneers: Andrew C. McBride, 25 Cloane Road

DUNGIVEN
Market held second Tuesday in the month
Local auctioneers: Frank Donaghy, Main Street

KILREA
Market day Wednesdays
Local auctioneers: H. A. McIlrath & Sons, Maghera Street

LIMAVADY
Market day Mondays
Local auctioneers: Alexander Love, 28 Main Street

MAGHERA
Market days Wednesdays and Fridays
Local auctioneers: J. Burns, 61 Main Street

MAGHERAFELT
Market days Wednesdays and Fridays
Local auctioneers: W. Gamble & Co, 43 Rainey Street

Tyrone

AUGHNACLOY
Market day Wednesdays

BALLYGAWLEY
Market day Fridays

CARRICKMORE
Market day Fridays

CASTLEDERG
Market held last Friday every month
Local auctioneers: Wm Carson, 8 Ferguson Crescent

CLOGHER
Market day Saturdays
Local auctioneers: Robert A. Noble, 4 Ashfield Road

COOKSTOWN
Market day Saturdays
Local auctioneers: John Keenan, 44 Greenvale Drive

OMAGH
Market held first Tuesday in the month
Local auctioneers: W. J. Anderson & Co, 6 Market Street

STEWARTSTOWN
Market held alternate Wednesdays